# Living Trust & Estate Planning for Seniors: A Step-by-Step Guide to Safeguarding Your Legacy and Loved Ones

Kai Pierce

# Table of contents

# Why Your Estate Plan Can't Wait

Margaret had always meant to get around to it.

She was 71, sharp as ever, and kept a running mental list of things she'd do "when things slowed down." Update her will—the one drafted in 1987, when her youngest was still in diapers. Set up that trust her accountant had mentioned twice. Write down which of her three children should inherit the lake house. She wasn't wealthy by any stretch, but she had a home, a modest retirement account, and forty years of accumulated life sitting in a two-car garage in suburban Ohio.

Then one Tuesday morning in February, Margaret had a stroke. She never regained full consciousness. She passed nine days later.

What followed was not the peaceful transfer of a mother's love to her children. It was seventeen months of probate court, $23,000 in legal and administrative fees, a family rift over who was promised the 1962 Epiphone guitar hanging in the basement, and a forced sale of the lake house at below-market value to cover estate debts—because no one had been legally designated to manage the property while the courts deliberated. Her eldest daughter, Susan, took unpaid leave from work to manage paperwork. Her son, David, hired his own attorney. Her youngest stopped returning calls entirely.

Margaret hadn't been neglectful or careless. She had simply believed she had more time.

Thousands of families repeat this story every single year, in every state, at every income level. Probate courts across the country process the estates of people who intended to plan, who thought about planning, who maybe even downloaded a form once and left it in a folder somewhere. The courts do not distinguish between neglect and good intentions. They move at their own pace—slowly, expensively, and without the personal context that would have made everything easier. The emotional cost, which no court filing captures, tends to run even higher than the financial one.

Here is something the legal and financial industries don't always say plainly: **you do not need to be wealthy to need an estate plan, and you do not need a law degree to create one.**

That sentence is the foundation of everything in this book.

The estate planning conversation has historically been framed around the ultra-wealthy—trusts as tax shelters for multimillion-dollar portfolios, attorneys billing by the hour for strategies most people will never need. That framing has done real harm. It has caused millions of ordinary adults to conclude that estate planning isn't for them, that it's too complicated, too expensive, or simply premature. For anyone over 55 who owns a home, has children or grandchildren, carries a retirement account, or simply has opinions about what happens to their belongings and their medical care—that conclusion is a costly mistake.

What you actually need is not complicated. A small set of well-crafted legal documents, understood clearly and kept up to date, will shield your family from the chaos that swallowed Margaret's. These documents are not exotic instruments. They are tools that have existed for generations, refined over decades of real-world use, and now more accessible than ever to ordinary people who simply take the time to understand them.

This guide does that translation work. Every chapter converts legal terminology into plain English, explains why each document matters in practical terms, and ends with a concrete action step you can take immediately—not eventually, not when things slow down.

---

The journey ahead moves through eight chapters, each building on the last.

We begin with the foundational documents: what a will actually does, where it falls short, and what a durable power of attorney and healthcare directive contribute to a complete plan. From there, we move into the living trust—arguably the most powerful tool available to adults who want to keep their affairs out of probate court and maintain control over what they've built. You'll learn how a trust works, how to fund it properly, and the specific mistakes that cause otherwise solid plans to unravel.

Later chapters address the human side of estate planning: how to have honest conversations with your family, how to account for blended families and complicated relationships, and how to think about digital assets—bank accounts, email archives, cryptocurrency, subscription services—that previous generations never had to consider. We close with a clear system for reviewing and updating your plan as your life continues to change, because a document written today and never revisited can become nearly as problematic as no document at all.

Every chapter ends with something actionable. Not a vague suggestion, but a specific, real step you can complete before the week is out.

Margaret's story didn't have to end the way it did. Yours doesn't either. The difference between those two outcomes is not luck, wealth, or professional expertise. It is simply a decision—made today, not later—to put the right documents in place.

That decision starts here.

# Chapter 1 — Understanding Wills, Trusts, and Probate

## 1.1 The Three Pillars—and Why One of Them Is a Courthouse

Most people, when they think about estate planning at all, think about a will. It's the document everyone has heard of, the one that appears in movies and television dramas, the one lawyers hand over in wood-paneled offices while grieving families sit in leather chairs. Write a will, the thinking goes, and your affairs are in order. Your wishes will be honored. Your family will be taken care of.

This belief is understandable. It is also incomplete in a way that causes real, preventable damage to families every year.

A will is not the end of the story. In most cases, it is closer to the beginning of a legal process that can take months or years, cost thousands of dollars, and expose your private financial affairs to public record. That process has a name: probate. And understanding what probate actually is—not in the abstract, but in the specific, procedural, courthouse-hallway sense—is one of the most important things you can do before signing any estate planning document.

Let's build from the ground up.

---

**What a Will Actually Does**

A will, formally called a last will and testament, is a legal document that records your instructions for what should happen to your property after you die. It names an executor—the person responsible for carrying out those instructions—and, if you have minor children, it designates a guardian who would care for them. In straightforward terms, a will is your voice speaking from the past into a future you won't be present for.

What a will does not do is transfer anything directly or automatically. This is the part most people miss.

When you die with a will, that document doesn't simply execute itself. It doesn't cause your bank account to flow into your daughter's name or your house to transfer to your son. A will is, at its core, a set of instructions addressed to a court. And before those instructions can be followed, the court has to verify that the document is valid, confirm that you were of sound mind when you signed it, establish that all debts and taxes have been accounted for, and formally authorize your executor to act. That verification process is probate.

The will triggers the process. The court controls the timeline.

**What Probate Actually Looks Like**

Probate is the legal mechanism through which a deceased person's estate is administered under court supervision. Every state has its own probate statutes, its own filing fees, its own timelines, and its own specific requirements—but the general shape of the process is consistent enough to describe.

When someone dies with a will, the executor named in that document must file it with the probate court in the county where the deceased lived. The court opens a case, publishes a legal notice to creditors (this is a formal requirement in virtually every state, and it establishes a window—often three to six months—during which creditors can make claims against the estate), inventories the assets, resolves outstanding debts, and eventually authorizes distribution of what remains to the beneficiaries named in the will.

During all of this, your executor has limited power to act without court approval. They generally cannot sell property, close accounts, or make distributions until the court authorizes each step. If your estate includes real estate in more than one state, the situation becomes more complicated still: a separate ancillary probate proceeding may be required in each state where property is held.

The timeline for a straightforward probate case in an uncomplicated estate runs anywhere from six months to a year. Cases involving real estate disputes, creditor claims, family disagreements, or simply an overloaded court docket can stretch to two or three years without unusual circumstances. Attorney fees and executor fees, which are often calculated as a percentage of the gross estate value rather than the net, routinely absorb three to eight percent of an estate's total value before a single dollar reaches a beneficiary.

And here is something worth sitting with: probate records are public. The inventory of your assets, the value of your home, the names and shares of your beneficiaries, the details of any disputes—all of it becomes part of the public court record. Anyone who wants to look can look.

None of this means probate is inherently corrupt or incompetent. It exists for legitimate reasons: to protect creditors, to prevent fraud, and to provide a supervised process for resolving disputes when families can't agree. The problem is that probate treats every estate as a potential dispute requiring oversight, even when your family is loving, your wishes are clear, and the last thing your survivors need is a year of legal procedure layered on top of their grief.

### What a Trust Is, and Why It Changes the Equation

A trust is a legal arrangement in which you transfer ownership of assets to a structure you control—during your lifetime, with full access and authority—and designate how those assets should be managed and distributed after your death, or if you become incapacitated before then.

The key word in that description is ownership. When you place an asset into a properly funded trust, legal title to that asset shifts from you as an individual to the trust itself. You typically serve as your own trustee while you're alive and capable, meaning you retain complete practical control. But because the asset is owned by the trust rather than by you personally, it does not become part of your probate estate when you die. It doesn't need court validation. It doesn't require a filing fee or a legal notice period. It transfers to your named beneficiaries according to the trust's terms, managed by the successor trustee you designated, on a timeline measured in weeks rather than months or years.

This is the functional difference that changes everything for most families.

A will says: here are my instructions; please ask the court to carry them out.

A trust says: here are my instructions; here is the person I've already authorized to carry them out; the court's involvement is not required.

Both documents express your wishes. Only one of them keeps those wishes out of a courtroom.

## How the Three Pillars Fit Together

Wills, trusts, and probate are not competing concepts. They are interconnected parts of a single system, and understanding how they interact is essential before deciding which tools belong in your own plan.

Probate is not a document—it's a process, one that your estate will go through unless you have taken specific legal steps to avoid it. A will, despite being the document most associated with estate planning, does not avoid probate; it governs what happens inside probate. A trust, when properly established and funded, is the primary tool for keeping assets outside of probate entirely.

Most complete estate plans include both. A living trust handles the bulk of significant assets—real estate, investment accounts, valuable personal property—and keeps them out of court. A will, sometimes called a pour-over will in this context, serves as a backstop: it catches any assets that weren't transferred into the trust during your lifetime and directs them there upon your death. Even in that case those assets may pass through a simplified probate process, but the core of the estate moves cleanly and privately through the trust.

The important point for now is this: a will alone is a plan for probate, not a plan to avoid it. For many families over 55—particularly those who own a home, have adult children as beneficiaries, or simply value privacy and speed—a will by itself leaves a significant gap between what they intended and what their family will actually experience.

The chapters ahead fill that gap. But filling it begins with understanding exactly what you're working with—and what each document can and cannot do on its own.

## 1.2 Wills and Trusts Side by Side — What Nobody Tells You Upfront

If you've ever sat across from a financial advisor or an estate attorney and walked away feeling like the conversation was designed to confuse rather than clarify, you're not alone. The comparison between a will and a living trust is one of those topics that professionals sometimes overcomplicate, either because the nuance genuinely matters or because complexity justifies fees. What follows is a plain-English breakdown of how these two documents actually differ, where each one earns its place, and why certain assumptions most people carry into this conversation turn out to be wrong.

**Cost: The Number That Surprises People**

The upfront cost of a will is lower than the upfront cost of a trust. A basic will can be drafted by an attorney for a few hundred dollars, and in some states, a simple handwritten will—called a holographic will—carries legal weight if properly executed. A revocable living trust, by contrast, typically costs more to establish: attorney fees for a complete trust package, including the trust document itself, a pour-over will, powers of attorney, and healthcare directives, generally range from around $1,500 to $3,500 depending on complexity and geography.

That upfront gap, however, inverts itself after death.

An estate passing through probate with only a will typically incurs attorney fees, executor fees, court filing fees, and administrative costs that together consume three to eight percent of the gross estate's value. On a $400,000 estate—a modest home and a retirement account, nothing extravagant—that range represents $12,000 to $32,000 paid to the process before a single dollar reaches a beneficiary. A trust, having already transferred assets outside of probate, avoids the bulk of those costs. The successor trustee can act immediately, without court authorization, and distributions can often be completed within weeks.

The will is cheaper to create. The trust is cheaper to use. For most families, the math favors the trust—provided it's funded correctly, a point we'll return to in detail in Chapter 3.

### Privacy: A Difference Most People Don't Consider Until It's Too Late

A will becomes a public document the moment it enters probate. Court filings are public records, which means the inventory of your assets, the identities of your beneficiaries, the value of your home, and the details of any disputes are visible to anyone who wants to search the record. In practical terms, this means nosy neighbors, estranged relatives, creditors, and occasionally scammers who monitor probate filings for exactly this kind of information.

A trust is a private document. It does not get filed with any court. Its terms, your asset values, your beneficiaries, and your distributions remain known only to the people you choose to tell. This distinction matters more than many people initially recognize, particularly if your estate involves unequal distributions among children, a beneficiary with creditor problems, or family dynamics you'd prefer not to air in a searchable courthouse record.

### Speed: What Grief Looks Like While Waiting for a Court

When someone dies with only a will, their executor cannot distribute assets until the probate court authorizes it. Depending on the state, the court docket, the complexity of the estate, and whether any creditors or family members raise objections, that authorization can take anywhere from several months to several years. During that window, surviving family members may be unable to access funds they need, sell property that is costing money to maintain, or settle affairs that require legal authority to act.

A trust eliminates that waiting period. The successor trustee—the person you named to take over when you die or become incapacitated—can step into their role immediately. No court petition. No notice period. No waiting for a judge's calendar to open up. The practical difference for a surviving spouse who needs access to household funds, or for an adult child managing a parent's affairs from another state, can be enormous.

## Flexibility and Control During Your Lifetime

One of the most persistent myths about trusts is that placing assets into one means giving up control of them. A revocable living trust works in exactly the opposite way. During your lifetime, you serve as your own trustee, with full authority to buy, sell, refinance, spend, or otherwise manage every asset in the trust exactly as you would have before. The word "revocable" means you can amend the trust, add or remove assets, change beneficiaries, or dissolve the entire arrangement at any point while you're alive and competent.

You are not giving anything away. You are reorganizing ownership in a way that serves your family better after you're gone.

The loss-of-control fear is one of the most common reasons people delay setting up a trust, and it is based on a confusion between revocable trusts—the kind used for estate planning by ordinary families—and irrevocable trusts, which do involve surrendering control and are used for specific tax or asset protection strategies. Unless your estate is large enough to trigger federal estate tax concerns, or you have particular Medicaid planning needs, the trust you're most likely to use gives up nothing while you're alive.

### Addressing the "Trusts Are Only for the Wealthy" Myth Directly

This is perhaps the most damaging misconception in estate planning, and it has kept countless ordinary families from using a tool that would have served them well.

The idea that trusts belong only to the wealthy likely traces back to the era when establishing and administering a trust was genuinely expensive and complex, or to the specific type of irrevocable dynasty trusts used to shield generational wealth from estate taxes. Neither of those contexts describes what a revocable living trust actually is for most people.

If you own a home, a trust is worth considering. Residential real estate is typically the largest asset in a middle-class estate, and it is also one of the most cumbersome assets to move through probate—subject to appraisals, creditor claims, and court-supervised sale restrictions that can delay distribution for a year or more. Keeping a home inside a trust means it transfers to your heirs cleanly, quickly, and privately.

If you have adult children you want to protect from unnecessary legal complexity, a trust is worth considering. If you have a blended family with competing interests, a trust is worth considering. If you simply want to ensure that the person you've chosen to manage your affairs can do so without petitioning a court while also managing their grief, a trust is worth considering.

The threshold for benefiting from a trust is not a million-dollar portfolio. It is a home, a family, and a preference for your wishes being carried out efficiently rather than bureaucratically.

## 1.3 Which Documents Do You Actually Need?

Understanding the difference between a will and a trust is useful. Knowing which combination fits your specific situation is what makes that understanding actionable. Estate planning is not one-size-fits-all, and the right document structure for a widowed homeowner differs meaningfully from what makes sense for a married couple with stepchildren or a single adult with a straightforward estate. What follows is a framework for identifying where you stand before you move into the chapters that explain how to build each component.

**If You Are Single With No Dependents**

A single adult with a modest estate—a home, a retirement account, perhaps a vehicle and personal property—can accomplish a great deal with a well-drafted combination of a revocable living trust, a pour-over will, a durable power of attorney, and a healthcare directive. The trust handles the assets; the pour-over will catches anything inadvertently left outside the trust; the power of attorney designates someone to manage your financial affairs if you're incapacitated but still living; and the healthcare directive records your medical wishes and names someone to make decisions on your behalf if you cannot.

Without dependents to provide for, your primary goals are avoiding probate, ensuring your assets reach the people you intend, and making certain someone you trust has legal authority to act if you become unable to manage your own affairs. A trust-centered plan accomplishes all three.

**If You Are Married**

Married couples have additional planning options and additional considerations. Assets held in joint tenancy with right of survivorship pass automatically to the surviving spouse outside of probate, which sometimes leads couples to conclude they don't need a trust. That conclusion holds up only as long as both spouses are living. The moment the first spouse dies, the jointly held assets consolidate in the survivor's name—and now the survivor has no joint owner to provide that automatic transfer at their own death. The estate sits exposed to probate unless other arrangements are in place.

A revocable living trust designed for a married couple typically holds shared assets during both lifetimes, allows either spouse to act as trustee, and provides clear instructions for distribution after both spouses have died. It can also include provisions for managing assets if one spouse becomes incapacitated before death—a scenario that joint tenancy does nothing to address.

**If You Have a Blended Family**

Blended families—those with children from prior relationships, stepchildren, or complex beneficiary arrangements—represent the situation where clear, legally precise documentation matters most and informal arrangements fail most spectacularly. The collision between a surviving spouse's natural instinct to control remaining assets and adult children from a prior relationship who feel entitled to their biological parent's share of the estate is one of the most common sources of estate litigation in the country.

A trust allows you to be precise in a way a will often cannot. You can specify that your spouse has use of the family home for their lifetime, with the property passing to your children upon the spouse's death. You can establish separate shares for biological and stepchildren with different terms for each. You can name an independent trustee to manage distributions if you're concerned that family relationships will complicate a family member's ability to act neutrally.

If your family is blended, generic planning is a risk. Specificity is your protection.

**If You Are Widowed**

A surviving spouse who has not updated their estate plan since their partner's death is in a particularly vulnerable position. Joint accounts have already consolidated. Beneficiary designations may still list the deceased spouse. A will written when both partners were alive may no longer reflect current wishes or current asset ownership. The practical effect of this mismatch can be as disruptive as having no plan at all.

For widowed individuals, a trust review—or a trust established for the first time—combined with a systematic audit of beneficiary designations across all accounts is typically the most urgent priority. Chapter 7 covers the review process in full, but if this description fits your situation, treat it as a flag worth acting on before you reach that chapter.

Wherever you find yourself in this framework, the goal of the chapters ahead is the same: to give you enough understanding to make informed decisions, enough practical guidance to take concrete steps, and enough confidence to stop treating estate planning as something to get around to eventually.

Eventually is a word that has cost too many families too much. The rest of this book is about replacing it with done.

# Chapter 2 — Building Your Revocable Living Trust

## 2.1 The People Inside Your Trust — And Why Each One Matters

A revocable living trust is, at its core, a legal relationship between people. Before you think about which assets go into it, which attorney drafts it, or what it costs to set up, you need to understand the human architecture that makes it work. Every trust involves a small cast of roles—some filled by the same person, some requiring careful thought about who in your life is the right fit. Get the roles right, and the trust functions exactly as intended. Miscast even one, and the entire structure can strain under pressure at precisely the moment your family needs it to hold.

There are four roles to understand: the grantor, the trustee, the successor trustee, and the beneficiaries. None of these terms should intimidate you. By the end of this section, each one will map directly onto someone you know.

**The Grantor: The Person Whose Plan This Is**

The grantor is you. This is the person who creates the trust, transfers assets into it, and establishes the terms under which it operates. Some documents use the words "settlor" or "trustor" interchangeably with grantor—they mean the same thing, and if you encounter any of those terms in a legal document, they all point back to the individual who decided to create the trust in the first place.

As the grantor of a revocable living trust, you retain significant authority over the arrangement during your lifetime. You can amend the trust's terms whenever you choose. You can add assets to it or remove them. You can change who the beneficiaries are, adjust the shares each person receives, or revoke the entire trust and start over. Nothing is fixed, nothing is surrendered, and nothing requires court approval to change while you remain alive and competent. The revocable nature of the trust is precisely what distinguishes it from the irrevocable arrangements used in more complex tax planning—and it's what makes this tool practical and approachable for the vast majority of people using it for everyday estate planning.

If you're married and creating a trust together with your spouse, both of you are grantors. You share authority over the trust during your joint lifetimes, and the document will specify what happens to that authority when the first of you dies.

One more thing worth noting: although the trust legally owns the assets you transfer into it, the IRS does not treat a revocable living trust as a separate tax entity during your lifetime. You continue to report income from trust assets on your own personal tax return, using your own Social Security number. There are no new tax returns to file, no separate tax identification number to obtain while you're alive and the trust remains revocable. For tax purposes, nothing changes.

---

**The Trustee: The Person Managing the Trust Right Now**

The trustee is the person responsible for managing the assets held inside the trust according to its written terms. In the vast majority of revocable living trusts created for estate planning purposes, the grantor and the initial trustee are the same person. You create the trust, you fund the trust, and you serve as your own trustee—

managing your own assets, just as you always have, with no meaningful change to your daily financial life.

This is a point worth emphasizing because it addresses one of the most common hesitations people bring to this conversation. Serving as your own trustee means your checking account, your investment portfolio, your home—all of these remain under your control. You sign documents, make decisions, buy and sell as you see fit. The only practical difference is that the title on certain assets reflects the trust's name rather than your personal name. A deed might read "Margaret A. Sullivan, Trustee of the Margaret A. Sullivan Revocable Living Trust dated March 14, 2024" rather than simply "Margaret A. Sullivan." Same person, same house, same authority—slightly different paperwork.

When a married couple creates a joint trust, both spouses typically serve as co-trustees during their lifetimes, each with full authority to act independently. Some couples prefer this arrangement because it ensures continuity if one spouse is temporarily unavailable or incapacitated; others prefer to designate one spouse as the primary trustee and the other as a backup. Either structure works; the choice depends on how you and your spouse naturally manage financial decisions.

The trustee's legal obligations under the trust are called fiduciary duties—a phrase that essentially means the trustee is required to act in the best interests of the beneficiaries and in strict accordance with the trust's written terms. When you are both grantor and trustee, this obligation primarily becomes relevant in the context of your successor trustee, who will inherit those duties when you no longer can.

## The Successor Trustee: The Person Who Steps In When You Can't

If the trustee role deserves careful thought, the successor trustee role deserves even more of it. This is the person—or institution—who takes over management of your trust when you are no longer able to serve as trustee yourself. That transition happens under one of two circumstances: your death, or your incapacity.

The incapacity piece is something many people overlook when they think about estate planning, because the conversation tends to focus so heavily on what happens after death. But a well-structured trust doesn't just govern the transfer of assets when you die—it also provides a mechanism for managing those assets if you suffer a stroke, develop dementia, or are otherwise unable to handle your own financial affairs while still living. Without a trust, a family in that situation often has to petition the court for a conservatorship or guardianship—a costly, time-consuming legal process that puts a judge in charge of decisions your family should be making. Your successor trustee steps into that gap cleanly, with legal authority already established, needing no court involvement.

Choosing the right successor trustee is one of the most consequential decisions in the entire estate planning process. The person you name will have real authority over real assets, and they will be exercising that authority during a period of stress—managing your financial affairs while you are either incapacitated or recently deceased, possibly while also grieving, possibly from a different city, possibly while managing their own family and professional responsibilities.

What you're looking for is a combination of qualities that don't always exist in the same person: trustworthiness, organizational competence, financial literacy, emotional steadiness, and enough time and proximity to actually do the work. In practice, most people name an adult child, a sibling, or a close trusted friend. Some people name a professional trustee—a bank trust department or a trust company—particularly when no family member feels like the right fit, when the estate is complex enough to require professional management, or when naming one family member over another would create friction.

A few practical points about naming your successor trustee that don't always come up in initial attorney consultations:

You can name more than one person to serve as co-successor trustees, though this arrangement works best when the individuals live near each other, communicate well, and are unlikely to disagree on significant decisions. Co-trustee arrangements can also slow down the administrative process, since both parties may need to sign documents jointly depending on how the trust is written.

You should always name at least one alternate successor trustee—a backup in case your first choice is unable or unwilling to serve when the time comes. The person you name today may predecease you, may develop health problems of their own, or may simply find themselves in circumstances that make serving as trustee impractical. An alternate ensures the trust doesn't stall while a court appoints a replacement.

And the successor trustee you name today is not a permanent appointment carved in stone. As your life changes—as children mature, as relationships shift, as the people around you demonstrate over time who is and isn't equipped for this kind of responsibility—you can update this designation simply by amending your trust. Many people revisit this choice every few years as part of a routine plan review.

**The Beneficiaries: The People Your Trust Is Ultimately For**

Beneficiaries are the people—or organizations—who receive the assets held in your trust after you die. This is the most straightforward role in the structure, but it still carries important nuances that affect how you designate beneficiaries and under what terms they receive their inheritance.

Most people name their spouse as the primary beneficiary, with children or other family members as contingent beneficiaries—those who inherit if the primary beneficiary has already died. In a trust, unlike a simple beneficiary designation on an insurance policy or retirement account, you can attach conditions and instructions to each beneficiary's share. You can specify that a child's inheritance should be held in trust until they reach a certain age. You can direct that funds be used only for education and health expenses for a grandchild who is still a minor. You can provide for a disabled family member in a way that preserves their eligibility for government benefits, through a structure called a supplemental needs trust that can be built directly into your revocable trust's terms.

Beneficiaries can also be charitable organizations. If you intend to leave a portion of your estate to a church, a hospital, a university, or any other nonprofit, naming them directly as a trust beneficiary is a clean, legally clear way to accomplish that.

What beneficiaries cannot do—and this is worth stating plainly—is override the trust's written terms. The trust document governs. Verbal promises, family understandings, handwritten notes left with personal belongings: none of these carry legal weight inside a trust administration. Whatever you intend, it needs to be written into the document. This is one of the clearest arguments for working with an estate planning attorney rather than relying on generic online templates that may not capture the specific language needed to honor your actual intentions.

The grantor, the trustee, the successor trustee, and the beneficiaries—these four roles are the skeleton of every revocable living trust. Everything else: the asset transfers, the distribution instructions, the contingency provisions, the tax considerations—is built on top of this framework. Before any of that structure can serve your family, you need to know who fills each seat at the table.

Take a moment before moving to the next section and actually think about the names. Who would you name as successor trustee today? Who are your beneficiaries, and are there conditions you'd want to attach to anyone's share? Write those names down somewhere. The exercise of putting them on paper often surfaces questions you didn't know you had—and those questions are exactly what the rest of this chapter is designed to help you answer.

## 2.2 Drafting the Trust — From Blank Page to Binding Document

Understanding the roles inside a trust is the foundation. Actually building the document is where that understanding becomes legally enforceable. The drafting process is less mysterious than most people expect, but it does require deliberate decisions at each stage—decisions that, once made and properly recorded, will govern how your assets are managed and distributed for years or decades after you're gone. Rushing through this stage, or relying on a generic template that doesn't account for your specific circumstances, is one of the most common reasons trust plans fail to perform as intended.

Here is what the drafting process actually involves, and where the decisions that matter most tend to cluster.

## Starting With the Right Help

A revocable living trust is a legal document, and while the internet offers dozens of fill-in-the-blank templates at low or no cost, the savings at the front end frequently generate expenses at the back end. Generic templates are built for generic circumstances. They don't account for the specific language your state requires for certain provisions to be enforceable, they don't prompt you to think through contingencies that an experienced attorney would flag, and they rarely include the kinds of nuanced distribution terms that make the difference between a trust that works cleanly and one that creates confusion for your successor trustee.

For most people creating a trust as part of a complete estate plan, working with an estate planning attorney represents a reasonable and worthwhile investment. The total cost for a comprehensive plan—trust document, pour-over will, durable power of attorney, and healthcare directive—typically falls in a range that is substantially less than what a single year of probate administration would cost on a modest estate. That comparison reframes the expense in the way it deserves to be framed: not as a legal fee, but as insurance against a much larger and more disruptive cost your family would otherwise absorb.

If cost is a genuine constraint, many bar associations maintain referral services for reduced-fee legal assistance, and some nonprofit organizations serving seniors offer estate planning clinics. The goal is to arrive at a document that reflects your actual situation, reviewed by someone who understands the law in your state.

### Deciding How Your Assets Will Be Distributed

Once the structural elements of the trust are established—the parties, the governing law, the trustee succession—the most consequential drafting decisions involve distribution: who gets what, when they get it, and under what conditions.

The simplest approach is an outright distribution, sometimes called a lump sum distribution, in which beneficiaries receive their full share of the trust assets immediately upon your death, with no conditions attached. This approach works well when your beneficiaries are financially responsible adults who won't be harmed by receiving a significant sum at once, and when your estate is straightforward enough that there's no particular reason to extend the trust's active management past the point of distribution.

The alternative is a staged or structured distribution, in which the trustee holds assets on behalf of beneficiaries and releases them over time or upon the occurrence of specific events. A common structure for beneficiaries who are young adults specifies that they receive a portion of their share at one age—say, twenty-five—another portion at thirty, and the remainder at thirty-five. This approach acknowledges that the person best positioned to receive and responsibly manage a significant inheritance at sixty-five may have a grandchild who is not yet equipped to handle the same responsibility at twenty-two.

Staged distributions don't require that you distrust your beneficiaries. They simply build in time and structure that protect people from the well-documented difficulties that can accompany sudden inheritance at any age. Many estate planning attorneys observe that their clients' children, who are themselves mature adults, specifically request that grandchildren's inheritances be structured this way—not as a vote of no confidence, but as a practical gift.

## Provisions for Minor Grandchildren

If you have grandchildren who are minors, or adult beneficiaries who may have minor children by the time your trust is administered, the distribution question becomes more urgent. Minors cannot legally receive or manage property directly in any state. If your trust simply names a minor grandchild as a beneficiary with no further instruction, a court will appoint a guardian of the property to manage those assets until the child reaches adulthood—reintroducing exactly the kind of court involvement a trust is designed to avoid.

The solution is to include a children's subtrust provision—sometimes called a minor's trust—directly within your revocable living trust. This provision directs your successor trustee to hold a minor beneficiary's share in a separate subaccount within the trust, managed according to specific instructions you write now, until the child reaches an age you designate. The trustee can be authorized to use those funds for the child's health, education, maintenance, and support during that period, with the remaining balance distributing outright when the child reaches the age you've specified.

You control the terms. If you want funds available for college tuition at eighteen but believe full distribution should wait until twenty-five, you can write exactly that. If you want the trustee to have discretion to release funds early for a documented emergency, that discretion can be built in. What you cannot do effectively is leave these decisions to chance or assume that a generic template will capture your intentions with the specificity they deserve.

## Provisions for Beneficiaries With Disabilities

If any of your beneficiaries receives needs-based government assistance—Supplemental Security Income, Medicaid, or similar programs—a direct inheritance can disqualify them from those benefits, sometimes for years, by pushing their countable assets above the program's eligibility threshold. A person with a disability who receives a $50,000 inheritance outright may lose their Medicaid coverage until those funds are spent down, often on the very care that Medicaid had been covering.

The tool designed specifically for this situation is a supplemental needs trust, sometimes called a special needs trust. When properly drafted, this type of trust holds assets for the benefit of the person with a disability in a way that supplements rather than replaces government benefits—paying for things those programs don't cover, like certain therapies, recreational activities, technology, and personal items, without disqualifying the beneficiary from ongoing program eligibility.

A supplemental needs trust can be established as a standalone document or incorporated as a subtrust provision within your revocable living trust, activated only if the relevant beneficiary is receiving qualifying government assistance at the time of your death. An experienced estate planning attorney will flag this issue and draft the appropriate language. If you're working without professional help and have a beneficiary with a disability in your life, this is the provision most likely to require professional review before the document is finalized.

## Clauses That Should Never Be Left Out

Every trust document should include a no-contest clause, which discourages beneficiaries from challenging the trust in court by forfeiting their inheritance if they file a legal challenge and lose. It should include a spendthrift clause, which protects a beneficiary's share from being claimed by their creditors before distribution—a protection that matters more than people expect when a beneficiary has financial difficulties, a pending lawsuit, or a divorce. It should specify the governing law of the state where you reside, name at least one alternate successor trustee, and include clear instructions for what happens if a beneficiary predeceases you.

It should also address what happens to the residue of the trust—the assets remaining after all specific distributions have been made—so that no asset is left in a legal gray area because the document didn't contemplate it.

None of these clauses are exotic. All of them are standard elements in a competent estate planning attorney's template. Their absence, however, is the fingerprint of a document that was assembled too quickly or without adequate review.

## 2.3 Funding the Trust — The Step That Makes Everything Else Work

A trust document sitting in a folder, unsigned by anyone, is just paper. A trust document properly signed, witnessed, and notarized, but never funded, is only slightly more useful. Funding is the process of transferring ownership of your assets from your name as an individual into the name of your trust—and it is the step that most people either skip entirely or complete only partially, often because no one explained clearly that the drafting and the funding are two separate tasks, both of which are required.

The problem this creates is straightforward: your trust can only govern assets it owns. Any asset that remains titled in your personal name at the time of your death falls outside the trust and into your probate estate, regardless of what the trust document says about it. A house deed that still reads "John T. Patterson" rather than "John T. Patterson, Trustee of the John T. Patterson Revocable Living Trust" is a house that will go through probate. A brokerage account that was never retitled is an account a court will need to authorize before your successor trustee can touch it.

This is not a hypothetical risk. It is one of the most common reasons trust plans fail in practice, and it is entirely preventable.

**Real Estate**

Transferring real estate into your trust requires preparing and recording a new deed—typically a grant deed or quitclaim deed, depending on your state—that conveys the property from you individually to yourself as trustee of your trust. This is not a sale. No money changes hands, no transfer taxes are triggered in most states, and the mortgage on the property, if one exists, is generally not affected. Federal law specifically protects homeowners who transfer property into a revocable living trust from having the transfer treated as a due-on-sale event by their lender.

The new deed must be signed, notarized, and recorded with the county recorder's office in the county where the property is located. If you own real estate in more than one county or more than one state, a separate deed is required for each property, recorded in the appropriate jurisdiction. This is one of the areas where working with an attorney or a title company familiar with your local requirements is worth the modest cost—recording requirements vary by county, and an improperly prepared deed can be rejected or, worse, accepted but legally defective.

Once the deed is recorded, the property is inside the trust. From that point forward, when you sell or refinance, the documents will reflect the trust's ownership, and you'll sign in your capacity as trustee rather than as an individual. The process is administratively slightly different from what you may be accustomed to, but it is not complicated, and title companies and lenders handle trust-owned property routinely.

**Bank and Financial Accounts**

Retitling bank accounts, savings accounts, and money market accounts into the trust's name requires a visit or a written request to your financial institution. Most banks have a specific process for this and will ask to see a copy of your trust document—or at minimum a certification of trust, which is a condensed summary document your attorney can prepare that confirms the trust's existence and your authority as trustee without revealing the full terms of the document.

Once the account is retitled, the trust becomes the account owner. You continue to use the account exactly as before: same checks, same debit card, same online access. Nothing about the operational experience changes. The difference appears only on the account's title paperwork and on the statement header.

Some people maintain one small personal checking account outside the trust for day-to-day convenience—this is a common and reasonable approach, provided the pour-over will is in place to capture that account's balance through a simplified probate process if needed.

**Investment and Retirement Accounts**

Brokerage and investment accounts follow a similar retitling process, handled through your broker or investment advisor. As with bank accounts, the account continues to function identically from your perspective once it's retitled. Dividends, interest, and capital gains continue to flow through on your personal tax return, because the trust remains a grantor trust for tax purposes during your lifetime.

Retirement accounts—IRAs, 401(k)s, 403(b)s—are a different matter, and this distinction is important enough to state plainly. You generally should not transfer ownership of a retirement account into your trust. Doing so can trigger immediate income tax consequences, as the transfer may be treated as a distribution subject to ordinary income tax. Instead, the appropriate approach for retirement accounts is to update the beneficiary designation on the account directly with the account custodian, naming the people or trust provisions you want to receive the funds after your death. Retirement accounts pass by beneficiary designation outside of probate, and that mechanism works cleanly without trust ownership.

Your estate planning attorney and financial advisor should coordinate on this point, because the interaction between trust planning and retirement account beneficiary designations is an area where decisions made in one domain can create unintended consequences in the other.

### Personal Property

Vehicles, jewelry, art, furniture, and other personal items present a different challenge. Most of these assets don't have formal title documents, which makes the retitling process less formal as well. Many trusts include a general assignment of personal property—a document that broadly transfers ownership of the grantor's tangible personal property into the trust—without requiring a separate transfer for each individual item. Vehicles with formal titles can be retitled through your state's department of motor vehicles, though some people leave vehicles outside the trust and handle them through other means, depending on their state's rules for small estate transfers.

The specific items that matter most—jewelry with significant value, art, collectibles, instruments—should be addressed explicitly in the trust's terms or in a separate written memorandum, both to clarify ownership and to express your wishes about who should receive them.

**Keeping the Funding Current**

Funding is not a one-time event. Every time you acquire a significant new asset—a vacation property, a new investment account, an inheritance of your own—you need to assess whether that asset should be transferred into the trust. Many people set up a trust, complete the initial funding process conscientiously, and then acquire new assets over the following years that never make it in. Those assets, if not addressed, pass through probate as surely as if the trust had never existed.

Building a habit of asking "does this belong in the trust?" each time you acquire something of significance is a simple discipline that protects everything else you've put in place. Chapter 7 returns to this habit as part of a broader framework for keeping your plan current—but the habit starts now, at the moment the trust is funded for the first time.

The trust you draft is only as powerful as the assets inside it. Funding completes the work that drafting begins. Without it, the most carefully written document in the world is an empty shell.

With it, everything your plan was designed to accomplish becomes possible.

# Chapter 3 — Drafting a Will That Works

## 3.1 The Pour-Over Will — Your Estate Plan's Safety Net

There is a version of estate planning that feels finished the moment the trust document is signed and the initial funding is complete. The trust exists, the assets are transferred, the successor trustee is named—what else could there be to do? This feeling of completion is understandable, but it rests on an assumption that the real world rarely honors: that every asset you ever own will find its way into your trust before you die.

It won't. Not because you'll be careless, but because life moves faster than paperwork.

You'll open a new savings account during a busy month and forget to have it retitled. You'll receive a small inheritance from a relative whose estate takes two years to settle, and the check will arrive in your name alone. You'll buy a piece of land on a handshake and a title transfer that never gets cross-referenced against your trust. You'll accumulate personal property—tools, equipment, a vehicle purchased late in life—that carries value but never gets formally assigned. None of this reflects negligence. It reflects the ordinary accumulation of a life that doesn't pause to consult your estate plan before each transaction.

This is the problem the pour-over will exists to solve.

---

**What a Pour-Over Will Actually Does**

A pour-over will is a specific type of last will and testament designed to work in direct coordination with a revocable living trust. Its central instruction is simple: any asset that you owned at the time of your death and that was not already held inside your trust should be transferred—poured over—into the trust upon your death, where it will then be distributed according to the trust's terms.

Think of your trust as a container you've built to hold and distribute your estate cleanly, privately, and without court involvement. The pour-over will is the mechanism that catches everything that missed the container and routes it there anyway. It doesn't create a parallel set of distribution instructions or establish a competing set of beneficiaries. It defers entirely to the trust, making the trust the single governing document for your entire estate, regardless of where individual assets happened to be titled when you died.

The drafting is typically straightforward. A pour-over will identifies you as the testator, names an executor responsible for carrying out its instructions, and includes the core directive: residue of the probate estate pours into the named trust. Most pour-over wills are relatively brief documents compared to a standalone will that must carry the full weight of an estate plan on its own, precisely because the trust is doing the heavy lifting.

### A Pour-Over Will Still Involves Probate

Here is the part of this arrangement that sometimes surprises people, and that deserves to be stated plainly rather than buried in a footnote: assets that pass through a pour-over will must still go through probate before they reach the trust.

The pour-over will is not a mechanism for avoiding probate. It is a mechanism for ensuring that assets which do end up in probate ultimately arrive at the right destination—your trust—rather than being distributed under generic state intestacy laws or through whatever outdated standalone will you might have otherwise left behind. The probate process for those assets will still take time, still involve court supervision, and still incur some administrative cost.

What this means practically is that the pour-over will functions best when it has very little work to do. A well-funded trust, conscientiously maintained over the years, leaves almost nothing outside its ownership at the time of death. The pour-over will becomes a procedural backstop for minor oversights rather than the primary vehicle for moving significant assets. In many estates administered through a well-funded trust, the pour-over will catches nothing at all—and that is exactly the outcome you're aiming for.

Some states have simplified probate procedures for small estates that fall below a certain dollar threshold, which means assets caught by a pour-over will may qualify for an expedited court process rather than full probate administration. California, for example, has a summary procedure for estates below a specified value, and many other states have analogous provisions. Your estate planning attorney can advise on the threshold in your state and how it might apply to any assets likely to end up outside your trust.

### Why You Need One Even If You Think Your Trust Is Fully Funded

The argument for including a pour-over will in every trust-based estate plan isn't complicated, but it's important enough to make explicitly. Even if you are meticulous about funding—even if you retitle every account, record every deed, and review your asset list annually—the pour-over will costs almost nothing to add to your plan and provides protection against scenarios you cannot fully anticipate.

Consider what happens if you die without a pour-over will and an asset is found outside your trust. In that situation, the asset becomes part of your intestate estate—meaning it is distributed according to your state's default inheritance rules, which follow a fixed hierarchy of family relationships and take no account of your actual wishes. Your state's intestacy statute doesn't know that you wanted your vintage guitar collection to go to your youngest child, or that you intended a specific account to fund your grandchildren's education. It distributes according to a formula, and that formula may bear no resemblance to the plan you spent time and money building.

The pour-over will prevents that outcome by ensuring that any asset found outside the trust after your death is directed toward the trust's distribution scheme rather than the state's. It is, in the clearest possible terms, the document that ensures your trust-based plan actually governs your entire estate rather than just the portion you remembered to transfer in time.

## The Pour-Over Will Also Covers Two Things the Trust Cannot

Beyond its function as a catch-all for untransferred assets, the pour-over will serves two additional purposes that a trust document, by its nature, cannot address.

The first is the nomination of a guardian for minor children. A trust governs property. It can hold funds for a minor child's benefit and direct how those funds should be managed and distributed, but it cannot designate who will have physical custody of a child if both parents die. Only a will can make that nomination. For grandparents raising grandchildren, for parents of minor children from a later-in-life relationship, or for anyone who has legal responsibility for a minor, this function alone justifies including a will in the plan regardless of how complete the trust appears to be. Courts are not bound by a guardian nomination—a judge will always make the final determination based on the child's best interest—but a clearly expressed nomination in a valid will carries significant weight in that determination and ensures your voice is part of the process.

The second function is the appointment of an executor. Even when the bulk of an estate passes through a trust and requires no probate administration, the pour-over will names the person responsible for managing the probate process for any assets that do require it. The executor has legal authority to gather those assets, pay outstanding debts and taxes from the probate estate, and transfer the residue to the trust. Without a named executor, the court will appoint an administrator—someone who may not be the person you would have chosen, and who may not share your priorities or your family's understanding of the situation.

### What Happens When There Is No Pour-Over Will

The absence of a pour-over will in a trust-based estate plan creates a gap that most people don't discover until it's too late to close. If you have a trust but no will of any kind, assets outside the trust at the time of your death pass under your state's intestacy laws with no mechanism to redirect them. The trust's carefully crafted distribution terms apply only to what the trust already owns. Everything outside it is governed by a statute that doesn't know you, doesn't know your family, and has no interest in honoring the spirit of the plan you built.

If you have an old will from before your trust was created—one that doesn't include pour-over language—that document may actually conflict with your trust rather than support it, directing assets to beneficiaries named in the will rather than routing them through the trust's terms. Outdated wills that coexist with newer trusts without coordination are a source of confusion in estate administration that experienced attorneys encounter regularly and that families experience as prolonged, expensive disputes.

The solution is to treat the pour-over will and the trust as a single integrated plan, drafted together, reviewed together, and updated together whenever significant life changes occur. Neither document is complete without the other. The trust does the work; the pour-over will ensures nothing escapes it.

This is the architecture of a plan that actually holds. The chapters ahead continue building it out, moving from the foundational documents into the additional layers—powers of attorney, healthcare directives, beneficiary designations—that complete the picture. But every layer rests on the same base: a funded trust and a pour-over will working in coordination, covering each other's gaps, leaving nothing to chance or to a courtroom.

## 3.2 Making It Legal — The Formalities That Determine Whether Your Will Holds Up

A will can express your wishes with perfect clarity, name exactly the right people, and reflect years of careful thought—and still be thrown out by a court if the document wasn't executed correctly. This is not a hypothetical risk confined to edge cases. Will contests based on procedural defects are among the most common reasons estates end up in prolonged litigation, and they are almost entirely avoidable. The legal requirements for a valid will are not complicated, but they are specific, and the specificity matters.

Understanding what makes a will legally enforceable is the difference between a document that protects your family and one that gives a court grounds to disregard it entirely.

**The Core Requirements: What Every State Demands**

Despite meaningful variation in how different states approach will execution, there is a baseline of requirements that applies broadly across the country. A valid will must generally be in writing, signed by the person making it, and witnessed by at least two people who observe the signing and add their own signatures to confirm it.

The writing requirement is straightforward: oral wills, sometimes called nuncupative wills, are recognized in only a small number of states and only under highly specific circumstances, typically involving imminent death and limited asset values. For any practical estate planning purpose, your will must be a written document.

The signature requirement means your own signature, applied at the end of the document, in a way that indicates your intent to authenticate everything that precedes it. Most states require that you sign in the presence of your witnesses—not before, not after, but while they are physically present and watching. Some states allow you to acknowledge a previously applied signature to witnesses rather than signing in front of them, but the safer and cleaner practice in every state is to sign while your witnesses are in the room.

The witness requirement is where people most often make mistakes that create problems later. Virtually every state requires at least two witnesses. Several states require two witnesses as a minimum but will accept three. The witnesses must generally be adults of sound mind who are present when you sign and who then sign the document themselves, typically in your presence and in each other's presence. The timing and sequence of these signatures matters: witnesses who sign at different times, in different locations, or without observing your signature may provide testimony that a court finds insufficient to establish proper execution.

The most important rule about witnesses, and the one most commonly violated by people who try to handle this process informally: your witnesses should not be beneficiaries under your will. Most states do not make an interested witness—one who stands to inherit—an automatic bar to the will's validity, but they do create complications. In some states, a bequest to a witness is voided, even if the rest of the will stands. In others, the interested witness's testimony about the circumstances of signing carries less weight if the will is challenged. The simplest protection against any of these complications is to use witnesses who have no financial stake in your estate whatsoever.

### Notarization and the Self-Proving Will

Notarization is not required for a will to be valid in most states—but it is strongly recommended, and here is why.

When a will is admitted to probate, the court needs to establish that it was properly executed. In the absence of a notarized affidavit, this typically requires tracking down the witnesses, obtaining their live testimony or sworn statements, and waiting for that process to complete. If a witness has died, moved away, or simply cannot be located years after the signing, the probate process becomes more complicated and potentially more expensive.

A self-proving will solves this problem in advance. A self-proving will includes a notarized affidavit, signed by you and your witnesses at the time of execution, that attests to the circumstances of the signing under penalty of perjury. When a self-proving will is admitted to probate, the affidavit substitutes for live witness testimony—the court accepts the notarized statement as sufficient evidence of proper execution without needing to locate anyone. Most states recognize self-proving wills, and the additional step of having a notary present at the signing costs almost nothing in time or money relative to the administrative simplification it provides.

The practical advice is this: arrange for a notary to be present at your will signing alongside your two witnesses. Sign the will in the presence of all three. Have everyone sign the self-proving affidavit at the same time. The entire process typically takes less than thirty minutes, and the document that results is as clean and court-ready as a will can be.

---

**State-by-State Variation: Where the Details Diverge**

While the core requirements above apply broadly, the specific rules in your state may add requirements, recognize alternative execution methods, or impose conditions that a generic national guide cannot capture in full. A few of the most significant areas of variation are worth understanding.

Holographic wills—handwritten wills that are entirely in the testator's own handwriting and signed, but not witnessed—are valid in roughly half of all states. They are not valid in the other half. Even in states that recognize them, holographic wills are prone to challenges based on questions about the testator's handwriting, mental capacity, and intent, and they lack the self-proving affidavit that makes a formally witnessed will so much easier to admit to probate. Treating holographic wills as an acceptable substitute for a properly executed document is a risk that rarely justifies itself.

Louisiana operates under a civil law system with will requirements that differ substantially from those in common law states. If you are a Louisiana resident, or if you own property in Louisiana, the specific execution requirements for that state deserve particular attention from your attorney.

Some states have adopted electronic will statutes that permit wills to be signed and witnessed digitally, a development that accelerated significantly in the wake of the pandemic. The enforceability and portability of electronic wills across state lines remains an evolving area of law, and relying on an electronic will without professional guidance introduces uncertainty that a traditionally executed paper document avoids.

The bottom line on state variation is not that you need to memorize the statutes of your jurisdiction—it is that you need to work with someone who has. Your estate planning attorney knows the specific requirements in your state and will structure the execution ceremony accordingly. If you're executing a will without professional assistance, the state bar's website or your county probate court's public resources can provide jurisdiction-specific guidance on execution requirements.

**A Note on Execution Ceremonies and Common Mistakes**

The signing of a will is not a casual administrative task. It is a legal ceremony with specific requirements, and the circumstances surrounding the signing can become relevant evidence if the will is ever challenged on grounds of undue influence or lack of capacity.

A few practices protect the integrity of the execution regardless of what state you're in. Sign at a time when you are alert, rested, and in good health—not during a hospitalization or a period of significant cognitive difficulty. Have witnesses who know you well enough to testify that you appeared to understand what you were signing and were acting of your own free will. Keep the signing environment free of pressure: ideally, no potential beneficiaries should be present in the room during the execution, so no one can later claim they were hovering over the process.

Date the will clearly, and include the city and state where it was signed. Store the original in a secure but accessible location—a fireproof home safe, a bank safe deposit box, or with your attorney—and ensure your executor knows where to find it. A will that cannot be located after death may be presumed by the court to have been intentionally revoked, even if that was never your intention.

## 3.3 Executors, Bequests, and Guardianship — The Decisions That Give Your Will Meaning

The legal formalities discussed above determine whether your will survives a court challenge. The decisions covered in this section determine whether it actually does what you intended. A will that is executed perfectly but populated with vague instructions, ill-chosen appointments, and unaddressed specifics will create almost as many problems as no will at all—just more expensive ones.

## Choosing Your Executor

The executor—called a personal representative in some states—is the individual responsible for carrying out the instructions in your will. In the context of a trust-based estate plan, the executor's job is primarily administrative: identifying assets that ended up outside the trust, paying the estate's outstanding debts and any taxes due, managing the probate process for those assets, and ultimately transferring the residue to the trust per the pour-over will's instructions. In estates where the trust is well-funded and little passes through the will, this is a relatively manageable role. In more complex situations, it can require sustained attention over many months.

The qualities that make a good executor overlap significantly with those discussed for successor trustees in Chapter 2: organizational reliability, financial literacy, emotional stability under pressure, and enough time and proximity to do the work. But the executor role has one additional dimension that the trustee role does not always share: the executor deals directly with creditors, government agencies, and the probate court, which requires a particular tolerance for bureaucratic process and official correspondence.

Name an alternate executor in case your first choice is unavailable or unwilling to serve. Whether the executor should be compensated—most states allow reasonable executor compensation paid from the estate—is a conversation worth having with your attorney and with the person you're considering naming, before the appointment is made rather than after.

## Specific Bequests: Getting the Details Right

A specific bequest is a gift of a particular item or sum to a named individual or organization. In a trust-based plan, most of your estate passes through the trust rather than through specific bequests in the will—but certain categories of property benefit from explicit direction that the trust's general distribution terms may not provide with adequate precision.

Personal property with emotional significance is the most common source of family conflict in estate administration, and it is frequently the category least carefully addressed in estate documents. The lake house triggers the legal dispute; the grandmother's pearl necklace triggers the lasting estrangement. When you have items whose sentimental value exceeds their monetary value—jewelry, furniture with family history, artwork, musical instruments, military memorabilia, handmade quilts—naming a specific recipient in your will or in an attached personal property memorandum removes any ambiguity about your intention.

Many states permit a separate personal property memorandum—sometimes called a tangible personal property list—that can be updated periodically without requiring a full will amendment. You can add items, remove them, and change recipients as your collection and your relationships evolve over time, as long as the will references the memorandum and the memorandum is signed and dated. This mechanism is particularly valuable for people with extensive collections of personal items, because it avoids the cost of re-executing the will each time you decide to redirect a specific piece.

Charitable bequests deserve the same specificity as personal property gifts. If you intend to leave a percentage of your estate, a specific dollar amount, or a particular asset to a charitable organization, name the organization precisely—using its full legal name, its tax identification number if you have it, and a brief description of the gift's purpose if you have a preference for how it should be used. Charitable organizations change their names, merge with other entities, and occasionally dissolve. Including enough identifying information that your bequest can be traced to the right organization, even if its name has changed slightly, protects your philanthropic intention from administrative confusion.

A lapsed bequest occurs when a beneficiary named to receive a specific gift predeceases you. Without an alternate named, the gift may fall into the residue of your estate and be distributed in ways you didn't intend. For each significant specific bequest, name an alternate recipient who takes the gift if the primary beneficiary cannot.

**Guardianship Nominations for Minor Dependents**

For anyone with legal responsibility for a minor child—whether as a parent, a grandparent with custody, or a guardian under an existing court order—the guardianship nomination in a will is among the most important decisions in the entire estate plan. It is also, for many people, the most emotionally difficult.

A guardian nomination is your formal expression to the court of who you believe should have physical custody and legal responsibility for your minor dependent if you die while they are still a minor. Courts are not bound by this nomination—a judge will evaluate the nominee's fitness and make a determination based on the child's best interest—but a clearly expressed nomination in a valid will carries genuine weight in that determination. Courts are not looking to override the wishes of a deceased parent or guardian; they are looking for guidance, and a thoughtful, clearly stated nomination provides it.

Choose someone whose values align with yours in the ways that matter most for raising a child. Consider their age, their health, their geographic location, their existing family responsibilities, and their relationship with the child. Consider also whether the person you'd trust most as a guardian is the same person you'd trust most to manage money—because they may not be, and if they're not, you can separate the roles. A guardian handles the child's physical care and upbringing. A trustee under your trust handles the financial assets set aside for that child. Naming different people to these roles, if different people are better suited to each, is not complicated and is often the right answer.

Have this conversation with the person you intend to name before the will is executed. A guardian nomination is a significant responsibility to place on someone without warning, and discovering it for the first time in a probate proceeding—while simultaneously absorbing the news of your death—is not the introduction to the role that serves anyone well.

By the time you have worked through the decisions in this chapter—execution requirements, executor selection, specific bequests, and guardianship nominations—the outline of a complete and functional will is in place. The document isn't a standalone plan; paired with your trust, your pour-over language, and the additional instruments covered in the chapters ahead, it becomes the backstop that ensures your entire estate is governed by intention rather than left to the default rules of a system that doesn't know your family.

That is what a will that actually works looks like. Not just signed, but complete.

# Chapter 4 — Powers of Attorney and Healthcare Directives

## 4.1 When You're Still Here But Can't Speak for Yourself

The conversation about estate planning almost always gravitates toward death. Which assets go where. Who inherits the house. How to keep things out of probate. These are legitimate and important questions, and the preceding chapters have addressed them in detail. But there is a scenario that statistically affects more families than sudden death, that creates more immediate financial disruption, and that a surprising number of otherwise thorough estate plans fail to address adequately.

That scenario is incapacity.

At some point, a meaningful percentage of adults over 55 will experience a period—sometimes brief, sometimes extended, sometimes permanent—during which they are unable to manage their own financial affairs. A stroke that affects cognition. A surgery with a longer-than-expected recovery. A progressive neurological condition that develops gradually over years. An accident that leaves someone physically incapacitated while their mind remains intact. The specific circumstances vary enormously, but the legal and practical problem they create is consistent: someone needs to pay the bills, manage the investments, deal with the IRS, handle the mortgage, and make dozens of other financial decisions that don't pause because the person usually responsible for them is temporarily or permanently unable to act.

Without a legal document authorizing someone to do that work, the people who love you most are legally powerless to help—no matter how obvious your wishes might seem, no matter how long they've been managing things informally alongside you, no matter how urgent the need.

That document is the durable financial power of attorney, and it may be the most immediately practical instrument in your entire estate plan.

**What a Power of Attorney Actually Is**

A power of attorney is a legal document in which one person—the principal—grants another person—the agent, sometimes called the attorney-in-fact—the legal authority to act on the principal's behalf in specified matters. The document defines the scope of that authority: what the agent can do, under what circumstances, and for how long.

The word "durable" is the critical modifier for estate planning purposes, and it changes everything about how the document functions. An ordinary power of attorney—one without the durable designation—becomes void the moment the principal becomes incapacitated. This seems counterintuitive until you understand the historical legal logic: a power of attorney was originally conceived as a delegation of authority by someone who was present and capable, and if that person lost capacity, the delegation was considered to lapse. The problem, obviously, is that incapacity is precisely the situation in which you most need someone else to act on your behalf. An ordinary power of attorney evaporates at the exact moment it would be most useful.

A durable power of attorney includes specific language—the exact wording required varies by state, but the effect is consistent—declaring that the document remains in effect even if the principal becomes incapacitated. This single modification transforms the instrument from a convenience tool into an essential component of incapacity planning. Your agent's authority doesn't lapse when you need it most. It persists, by design, through exactly the circumstances the document was created to address.

### What Your Agent Can Actually Do

The scope of authority granted in a durable financial power of attorney can be broad or narrow depending on how the document is drafted. A general durable power of attorney typically grants the agent authority across the full range of financial matters: paying bills and managing household expenses, accessing and managing bank accounts, buying and selling real estate and other property, managing investment portfolios and retirement accounts, filing tax returns and dealing with the IRS, handling insurance claims and policy management, operating a business if the principal owns one, making gifts on the principal's behalf within specified limits, and managing loans, mortgages, and other debt obligations.

This is substantial authority, and its breadth is intentional. A narrow power of attorney that limits the agent to a short list of specific transactions may fail to cover something urgent that no one anticipated. Financial life is complicated and unpredictable, and an agent who discovers that their authority doesn't extend to the specific transaction the situation requires—a Medicaid application, a property refinance, a tax dispute—faces the same legal impasse as if no power of attorney existed.

Some people are uncomfortable granting such broad authority and prefer a limited power of attorney that restricts the agent to specific types of transactions. This is a legitimate choice, but it requires careful thought about what you might actually need an agent to handle and a willingness to accept the risk that the document won't cover every situation that arises. For most incapacity planning purposes, a broad general power of attorney with appropriate safeguards—discussed below—serves families better than a narrow one that creates gaps at inconvenient moments.

**The Alternative Is a Courtroom**

It is worth spending a moment on what happens when someone becomes incapacitated without a durable power of attorney in place, because the alternative clarifies why the document matters so urgently.

When an incapacitated adult has no legally authorized agent, and decisions need to be made about their finances, family members have one option: petition the court for a conservatorship, sometimes called a guardianship of the estate. A conservatorship is a court-supervised arrangement in which a judge appoints someone—typically a family member, though not always—to manage the incapacitated person's financial affairs under ongoing judicial oversight.

The conservatorship process is expensive to initiate, often requiring attorney fees, court filing costs, medical evaluations, and formal hearings. Once established, it requires regular reporting to the court: annual accountings of every financial transaction made on the incapacitated person's behalf, ongoing judicial approval for certain types of transactions, and continued legal fees for as long as the conservatorship remains active. The conservator may be required to post a bond. The proceedings are part of the public court record.

Beyond the financial cost, the conservatorship process takes time—weeks or months in many jurisdictions—during which urgent financial needs may go unmet because no one has legal authority to address them. A surviving spouse who needs to access a joint investment account to cover household expenses, an adult child trying to pay a parent's mortgage to prevent foreclosure, a family trying to manage a parent's rental property during a health crisis: all of these situations can be frozen in legal limbo while a court slowly authorizes the authority that a durable power of attorney would have provided immediately.

Perhaps most significantly, conservatorship removes the incapacitated person's ability to choose who manages their affairs. You've spent years observing the people in your life, assessing their judgment, watching how they handle responsibility and pressure and money. A durable power of attorney lets you act on that observation by naming the person you've concluded is actually right for this role. A court, making a conservatorship appointment without your input, may reach a different conclusion—or may simply default to whoever filed the petition first.

## Choosing Your Agent: The Most Consequential Decision in the Document

The legal mechanics of a durable power of attorney are relatively standardized. The decision that carries the most real-world consequence is the one that no form can make for you: who to name as your agent.

Your agent will have access to your financial life in a way that almost no one else does. They will be able to make transactions, sign documents, access accounts, and manage assets in your name. The scope of their authority, in a broad general power of attorney, extends to virtually everything of financial significance that you own. This is not a role to fill with the first available family member or the person who asks most enthusiastically.

The qualities that matter most in an agent are, in roughly this order: absolute trustworthiness, financial competence, organizational reliability, and availability. Trustworthiness sits at the top of that list not as a formality but because financial elder abuse—the misuse of a power of attorney to divert a principal's assets for the agent's own benefit—is among the most common forms of elder abuse reported in the country, and the perpetrators are frequently family members. Naming someone you trust without reservation, and putting in place the safeguards discussed below, is the primary protection against this risk.

Financial competence matters because your agent may need to make investment decisions, handle tax matters, negotiate with creditors, or manage a rental property—tasks that require more than good intentions. A devoted family member who is financially disorganized in their own life may struggle to manage your affairs competently under the stress of an incapacity situation. This is a case where love and capability are separate considerations, and both need to be present.

Availability is practical but essential. An agent who lives across the country, carries a demanding professional schedule, and has three young children may be the right person in terms of character and competence but may face genuine logistical obstacles to serving effectively. Think about who can actually do this work, not just who you'd most like to name.

Name an alternate agent—a backup who assumes authority if your primary agent is unwilling or unable to serve. The same life changes that make an alternate successor trustee necessary apply here: illness, death, geographic relocation, relationship changes.

An alternate costs nothing to name and prevents the document from becoming useless if the primary agent is unavailable.

## Safeguards That Belong in the Document

A well-drafted durable power of attorney is not simply a blank check of authority. It includes provisions that protect you from misuse while preserving your agent's ability to act effectively when needed.

One common safeguard is a requirement that the agent keep detailed records of all transactions made on the principal's behalf. Some documents require the agent to provide periodic accountings to a third party—a sibling, a trusted advisor, an attorney—creating a layer of oversight without requiring court involvement. Some principals include specific prohibitions: restrictions on gifts to the agent personally, limits on the agent's ability to change beneficiary designations, or requirements that major transactions be approved by a second person.

A springing power of attorney is another option: a document that does not take effect immediately upon signing but springs into effect only upon a defined triggering event, typically a physician's written certification that the principal is incapacitated. This approach appeals to people who are uncomfortable with the idea of their agent having active authority before incapacity actually occurs. The tradeoff is that in a sudden emergency, obtaining the physician's certification may introduce delay at a moment when speed matters. Many estate planning attorneys recommend an immediately effective durable power of attorney paired with the trust's own incapacity provisions, rather than a springing document, because the combination provides faster access to authority without meaningful additional risk.

What every durable power of attorney needs, regardless of its specific provisions, is proper execution under the laws of your state. Most states require the principal's signature to be notarized, and some additionally require witnesses. The execution requirements for powers of attorney differ from those for wills, and they differ by state—another reason to finalize these documents with professional guidance rather than generic online templates.

The durable financial power of attorney is not a dramatic document. It doesn't distribute assets, establish trusts, or nominate guardians. What it does is keep your financial life functional during a period when you can't manage it yourself—and it does that by giving someone you trust the legal standing to act that the law otherwise reserves exclusively for you. For every family that has watched a parent's finances deteriorate during a medical crisis while they were legally powerless to intervene, the value of that document is not abstract. It is measured in the specific, urgent, expensive problems it would have prevented.

## 4.2 Healthcare Directives — Putting Your Medical Wishes in Writing Before Someone Else Has To

Financial incapacity is disruptive. Medical incapacity is something else entirely. When a person loses the ability to make or communicate their own healthcare decisions—whether suddenly, through accident or cardiac event, or gradually, through the progression of a neurological condition—the people around them are thrust into one of the most emotionally difficult situations a family can face. They are grieving, frightened, and exhausted, often in a hospital waiting room, and they are being asked to make decisions about ventilators, feeding tubes, surgical interventions, and end-of-life care that they may have no idea how to answer.

Without clear documentation of your wishes, those decisions don't belong to the people who know you best. They belong to the medical system's default protocols, interpreted by clinicians who have never met you, modified by whoever in your family speaks most forcefully or most often, and occasionally resolved by a court when family members cannot agree. The healthcare directive exists to prevent that outcome by ensuring your voice is present in those conversations even when you cannot speak for yourself.

There are two distinct documents that together constitute a complete healthcare directive, and understanding what each one does—and why both are necessary—is the starting point for this part of your plan.

### The Living Will: Your Instructions to the Medical System

A living will, sometimes called an advance directive or directive to physicians, is a written statement of your wishes regarding specific types of medical treatment in specific circumstances. It speaks directly to clinicians rather than to a person: it tells your medical team what interventions you do and do not want if you are in a defined medical condition and cannot communicate your preferences.

The circumstances a living will typically addresses are those involving terminal illness, permanent unconsciousness, or end-stage medical conditions from which no meaningful recovery is expected. Within those circumstances, the document records your position on a range of interventions: cardiopulmonary resuscitation, mechanical ventilation, artificial nutrition and hydration, dialysis, antibiotics and other infection-fighting treatments, and comfort-focused care—the medical approach that prioritizes pain management and quality of remaining life over curative intervention.

The value of recording these preferences in advance is not primarily legal, though the legal recognition is important. The value is that it removes an impossible burden from the people who love you. When a physician approaches a family and asks whether a patient on a ventilator who has not shown brain activity in five days should remain on life support, that question lands differently depending on whether the family has a document expressing the patient's own position. Without that document, the family is making a decision that will live with them forever, often without knowing what the person actually wanted, frequently in disagreement with each other, and sometimes in conflict with the medical team's assessment. With the document, they are honoring a decision their loved one already made. The emotional weight is different in kind, not merely in degree.

Living wills are most useful when they are specific. A document that says only "I do not want extraordinary measures" gives clinicians and family members limited guidance, because "extraordinary" is a judgment call that different people make differently. A document that specifies "if I am in a persistent vegetative state with no reasonable expectation of recovery, I do not wish to be kept alive by mechanical ventilation or artificial nutrition" gives the medical team and your family a clear, actionable instruction that leaves far less room for interpretation or dispute.

State forms for living wills are available through state health departments, bar associations, and many hospital systems, and they are designed to meet the specific legal requirements of their jurisdiction. Using your state's form, or a document drafted with attention to your state's requirements, ensures the document will be recognized by healthcare providers in your area.

## The Medical Power of Attorney: Your Voice in the Room

A living will addresses specific medical scenarios in advance, but medicine doesn't always present itself in the scenarios you anticipated. There will be decisions your living will didn't cover—treatment choices, care settings, surgical options, rehabilitation plans—where someone needs to speak on your behalf in real time. That is the function of the medical power of attorney, sometimes called a healthcare proxy or healthcare power of attorney depending on the state.

The medical power of attorney designates a specific person—your healthcare agent—to make medical decisions on your behalf when you are unable to make or communicate them yourself. Unlike the living will, which operates as a pre-recorded set of instructions, the medical power of attorney operates through a person: someone who knows you, understands your values, and can engage dynamically with physicians, weigh options, and make judgment calls in situations no document could fully anticipate.

The authority granted to a healthcare agent is broad by design. They can consent to or refuse treatments, choose between surgical options, decide where you receive care—hospital, rehabilitation facility, home hospice—authorize the release of medical records, and in some states, make decisions about organ donation. In the most serious circumstances, they may need to decide whether to continue or discontinue life-sustaining treatment if your living will's language doesn't clearly resolve the situation at hand.

This is profound authority to place in another person's hands, and the choice of healthcare agent deserves the same serious consideration given to successor trustee and financial agent selections—perhaps more, because the decisions your healthcare agent makes cannot be undone.

The right healthcare agent is not necessarily the person closest to you emotionally. It is the person who can hold your interests steady under acute stress, who can advocate firmly with medical professionals without becoming confrontational, who can make a difficult decision and accept the weight of it, and who will honor what you actually wanted rather than what they wish you had wanted. These qualities sometimes describe a spouse or an adult child. They sometimes describe a close friend who has witnessed you navigate health challenges before. They occasionally describe a professional patient advocate. What matters is an honest assessment of who in your life actually fits this profile, rather than who it would feel most natural to name.

If you are married, naming your spouse as healthcare agent is intuitive and often appropriate—but consider whether your spouse would be able to function effectively in this role during a medical crisis, or whether they would be so overwhelmed by their own fear and grief that their judgment would be compromised. Some couples name each other as primary agent with an adult child as alternate for exactly this reason: the adult child may be more capable of maintaining clarity during a crisis precisely because they have slightly more emotional distance.

---

**Real Scenarios: Where These Documents Do Their Work**

Consider three situations that play out in hospitals and care facilities every day, and how the presence or absence of healthcare directives changes the outcome.

In the first situation, a 74-year-old man suffers a massive stroke and is placed on a ventilator in the emergency room. He has no living will and no healthcare agent designated. His two adult children disagree about whether he would have wanted to be kept on life support—one believes he would have wanted every possible intervention, the other recalls a conversation years earlier in which their father said clearly he never wanted to live "attached to machines." The hospital ethics committee is eventually convened. The process takes weeks. The family relationship does not recover.

In the second situation, the same man has a living will that states he does not wish to be maintained on mechanical ventilation if he has suffered a neurological event with no reasonable expectation of meaningful recovery, and a medical power of attorney naming his daughter as healthcare agent. The daughter meets with the neurologist, reviews the prognosis, and makes the decision consistent with her father's written wishes. It is still devastating. But it is not a dispute. It is an act of honoring someone's life rather than fighting over its end.

In the third situation, a 68-year-old woman is diagnosed with early-stage dementia. While she still has full decision-making capacity, she works with her physician and her estate planning attorney to document her healthcare preferences in detail: her wishes regarding memory care placement if she can no longer live independently, her preferences about resuscitation as the disease progresses, her position on hospitalization in the final stages of illness. Her healthcare agent—her sister—receives a copy of everything and has a long conversation with her about the reasoning behind each decision. Years later, when the time comes to make those decisions, the sister knows exactly what her role is and what her sister wanted.

The document doesn't eliminate grief. It does eliminate ambiguity, and in a medical context, ambiguity costs families dearly.

**HIPAA Authorization: The Overlooked Companion Document**

One document that often gets omitted from the healthcare directive conversation, despite being practically essential, is a HIPAA authorization. Federal medical privacy law restricts what healthcare providers can share about a patient's condition with anyone other than the patient—including family members—without written authorization. Even a named healthcare agent may encounter resistance from hospital staff sharing information if the HIPAA authorization is not clearly documented.

Including a signed HIPAA release that specifically authorizes your healthcare agent and any other family members you designate to receive medical information ensures that the people who need to be informed can actually be informed. Without it, your healthcare agent may find themselves trying to make decisions with incomplete information because a nurse or administrator is adhering—correctly, under the law—to privacy protocols.

## 4.3 Making Sure Your Documents Are There When They're Needed

A power of attorney that sits in a filing cabinet no one knows about is, in a practical emergency, nearly useless. A healthcare directive that exists only as a digital file on a password-protected computer is inaccessible to the paramedics arriving at your home. The most carefully drafted, properly executed set of estate planning documents can fail at the critical moment not because of any legal deficiency but because of a simple logistical one: no one could find them fast enough.

Accessibility is not an afterthought in estate planning. It is a design requirement.

## Choosing Agents Who Are Actually Reachable

Before addressing where documents should be stored, there is a prior question that the selection of agents raises: are the people you've named reachable when needed? An agent who travels internationally for work, who regularly goes off the grid on extended trips, or who lives in a different time zone from your primary physicians introduces logistical challenges that a backup agent can resolve. Your primary agent for both financial and healthcare matters should be someone who can be reached quickly in an emergency and who can respond without days of delay.

Talk to every person you've named—primary and alternate—before finalizing your documents. Confirm they are willing to serve, understand the responsibilities involved, and know where your documents are located. An agent who discovers their role for the first time in an emergency room or probate proceeding is starting from a significant disadvantage. An agent who has read the document, discussed it with you, and knows where the original is stored can act immediately.

## Setting Limits That Reflect Your Actual Concerns

Both financial and healthcare agents can be given broader or narrower authority depending on your comfort level and your specific situation. For financial agents, common limitations include restrictions on the agent's ability to make gifts to themselves, requirements that they provide periodic accountings to a designated third party, and prohibitions on changing your estate planning documents or beneficiary designations. These limits don't impede the agent's ability to manage your affairs effectively—they simply close off the specific avenues through which financial elder abuse most commonly occurs.

For healthcare agents, you can specify in the medical power of attorney which types of decisions require the agent to attempt to reach you first, even if your capacity is limited. You can require that the agent consult with specific family members before making major decisions, without giving those family members actual veto power. You can specify that the agent's authority is limited to situations where two physicians have independently certified your incapacity, rather than taking effect based on the agent's own assessment.

None of these limitations are mandatory, and none of them are appropriate in every situation. What makes them worth considering is that they reflect your actual concerns about how authority might be misused, and addressing those concerns explicitly in the document is far more effective than worrying about them privately after signing.

## Where Documents Should Live — And Who Should Know

Original documents have legal significance that copies often don't. Your original durable power of attorney, your original healthcare directive, and your original living will should be stored somewhere secure but accessible—not locked in a safe deposit box that requires a court order to open after your death, and not buried in a filing system that only you understand.

A fireproof home safe with the combination or key held by your agent is a practical option. Leaving originals with your estate planning attorney, who maintains a document storage system and can release them to the appropriate person upon request, is another. Some states maintain advance directive registries where you can file your healthcare documents for retrieval by medical providers. Hospitals in many areas ask patients to provide copies of healthcare directives at admission, and keeping a copy in your medical file with your primary care physician ensures it's accessible to any provider who treats you through that practice.

Critically, your healthcare agent should have a copy of your living will and medical power of attorney—not just knowledge of their existence, but an actual copy they can hand to a clinician in an emergency. Your financial agent should have a copy of the durable power of attorney. First responders and emergency room staff cannot wait for documents to be retrieved from a storage location; they need to see the document now.

## The Critical Contacts Summary: One Page That Ties Everything Together

Every complete estate plan benefits from a single summary document—one page, plain language, no legal jargon—that tells the people responsible for your affairs exactly where everything is and who to call. This document isn't a legal instrument; it doesn't need to be notarized or witnessed. It is simply a practical guide written for the person who will be managing a crisis without enough information.

That summary should include your full legal name and date of birth, the location of your original estate planning documents including the trust, will, powers of attorney, and healthcare directives, the names and contact information for your estate planning attorney, your financial advisor, your accountant, and your primary care physician, the names and contact information for your successor trustee, executor, financial agent, and healthcare agent, the institutions where your financial accounts are held with approximate account types but not full account numbers, the location of your safe deposit box and the location of the key, your insurance policies and the contact information for each insurer, and any digital account information stored in a password manager with instructions for accessing it.

Store this summary with your estate planning documents and give a copy to your successor trustee and your primary agents. Review it annually and update it whenever something on the list changes. It costs nothing to create and requires no professional assistance to maintain—but for the person stepping into your affairs during a crisis, it can compress weeks of frantic searching into a single organized starting point.

The documents discussed in this chapter and throughout this book are only as powerful as the systems that make them findable and usable. Building those systems is the last act of clarity in an estate plan—the step that ensures everything you've put in place actually reaches the people who need it, at the moment they need it most.

# Chapter 5 — Protecting Assets from Taxes and Creditors

## 5.1 Understanding Your Tax Exposure — What the Government Can Actually Claim

Few topics in estate planning generate more confusion, more anxiety, and more misplaced urgency than taxes. The words "estate tax" land differently than they should for most people—conjuring images of the government claiming a substantial portion of everything a person spent a lifetime building, leaving heirs with a fraction of what was intended. That image is not inaccurate for a specific category of very large estates. For the vast majority of Americans over 55, however, it describes a threat that simply doesn't apply to their situation, and the anxiety it generates can distort planning priorities in ways that cost more than the taxes being feared.

The goal of this section is not to minimize legitimate tax concerns where they exist. It is to give you an accurate picture of where the actual thresholds are, what triggers tax exposure, and how much of your estate is genuinely at risk—so that your planning energy goes toward the real vulnerabilities in your specific situation rather than toward scenarios that don't apply to you.

### The Federal Estate Tax: Who Actually Pays It

The federal estate tax is a tax imposed on the transfer of wealth from a deceased person's estate to their heirs. It applies only to the portion of an estate that exceeds the applicable exemption amount—the threshold below which no federal estate tax is owed at all. Understanding where that threshold sits, and what it means for your estate, is the starting point for any honest conversation about federal tax exposure.

As of the time this book went to press, the federal estate tax exemption stands at approximately $13.61 million per individual, a figure adjusted periodically for inflation. A married couple can effectively combine their exemptions through a legal mechanism called portability, which allows a surviving spouse to use the unused portion of a deceased spouse's exemption in addition to their own—bringing the combined threshold for a married couple to roughly $27 million before federal estate tax applies to any part of their estate.

Those numbers deserve a moment of reflection, because they reframe the conversation entirely for most readers. If your estate—including your home, retirement accounts, life insurance death benefits, investment accounts, business interests, and personal property—totals less than $13.61 million as an individual or less than $27 million as a married couple, your estate currently owes no federal estate tax whatsoever. Not a reduced amount. Not a percentage of the excess. Nothing.

By the Internal Revenue Service's own estimates, federal estate tax affects fewer than one in a thousand estates in any given year. The people for whom federal estate tax is a genuine and immediate planning concern represent a very small slice of the population, and they almost certainly already have professional advisors addressing it. If you are reading this book to build a foundational estate plan for a middle-class or upper-middle-class estate, federal estate tax is likely not your primary concern—and treating it as though it were can lead to unnecessary complexity, cost, and distraction from the planning that actually matters for your situation.

That said, there is a significant caveat that every reader in the current environment should understand. The elevated exemption amounts in place at the time of publication were established by the Tax Cuts and Jobs Act of 2017, and absent further congressional action, they are scheduled to revert to approximately half their current level—roughly $7 million per individual, adjusted for inflation—after December 31, 2025. For estates that currently sit well below any threshold of concern, this sunset provision may remain irrelevant. For estates in the $7 to $14 million range, however, the potential halving of the exemption creates a planning window that is worth discussing with a qualified estate planning attorney or tax advisor before the provision takes effect.

Tax law changes. The figures cited here reflect the law as understood at the time of writing, and any reader whose estate approaches the threshold—or who anticipates significant asset growth through business sale, inheritance, or real estate appreciation—should verify current figures with a professional rather than relying on any book's static numbers.

### State-Level Estate and Inheritance Taxes: The Hidden Exposure

The federal exemption threshold reassures most people. What reassures them somewhat less, once they understand it, is that federal estate tax is not the only tax that can apply to a transferred estate. A number of states impose their own estate or inheritance taxes, often with exemption thresholds far below the federal level—and for residents of those states, the state-level tax represents a genuine planning consideration even for estates that fall nowhere near the federal threshold.

It is important to distinguish between two types of state-level transfer taxes, because they operate differently and affect different people.

A state estate tax is imposed on the estate itself—on the total value of the assets being transferred, assessed before distribution to heirs. It functions similarly to the federal estate tax in structure, applying to the portion of the estate that exceeds the state's own exemption. The states that currently impose an estate tax include Oregon, Washington, Minnesota, Illinois, Massachusetts, Maryland, Vermont, Connecticut, Hawaii, Maine, New York, and the District of Columbia, among others, and each sets its own exemption amount and rate structure. Massachusetts and Oregon, for example, have historically maintained estate tax exemptions as low as $1 million—a threshold that a home, a modest retirement account, and some savings can approach without difficulty in many parts of those states.

An inheritance tax operates differently. Rather than taxing the estate before distribution, an inheritance tax is imposed on the beneficiary who receives the assets, based on the value of what they receive and their relationship to the deceased. The states that currently impose an inheritance tax include Iowa, Kentucky, Maryland, Nebraska, New Jersey, and Pennsylvania. Maryland is notable for imposing both an estate tax and an inheritance tax, making it one of the more complex state-level tax environments for estate planning purposes.

The relationship between the beneficiary and the deceased typically determines both whether the inheritance tax applies and at what rate. Surviving spouses are exempt from inheritance tax in every state that imposes it. Children and direct descendants are often exempt or taxed at low rates. More distant relatives—siblings, nieces and nephews, cousins—and unrelated beneficiaries typically face higher rates that can range from several percent to fifteen or eighteen percent of the value received, depending on the state.

If you live in a state that imposes either type of tax, or if you own property in such a state, the state-level tax exposure should be an explicit part of your planning conversation. For a Massachusetts resident with an estate of $1.5 million—entirely plausible for a homeowner with a retirement account and some savings—the state estate tax applies to the excess above the exemption even though the federal tax doesn't apply at all. The liability is real, and there are legitimate planning strategies for addressing it, including irrevocable trust structures, charitable giving, and lifetime gifting programs.

**The Gift Tax: What It Is and How It Interacts With Your Estate**

The federal gift tax is closely linked to the estate tax through what is called the unified credit—a single lifetime exemption that applies to both taxable gifts made during your lifetime and the value of your estate transferred at death. Understanding this connection clarifies both why the gift tax exists and how it affects common planning strategies.

The basic mechanics work as follows. The same $13.61 million lifetime exemption that applies to your estate also applies to taxable gifts you make while living. If you give away $1 million during your lifetime in amounts that exceed the annual gift tax exclusion, that $1 million reduces your remaining estate tax exemption dollar for dollar. The unified credit prevents wealthy individuals from avoiding estate tax simply by distributing assets before death.

The annual gift tax exclusion is a separate, independent allowance that sits outside the unified credit and does not reduce your lifetime exemption at all. As of publication, any individual can give up to $18,000 per year to any number of recipients without triggering a gift tax filing requirement or reducing their lifetime exemption. A married couple can combine their exclusions to give $36,000 per year to each recipient through a process called gift splitting. These annual exclusion gifts are a clean, simple mechanism for reducing the size of an estate over time, and for estates that approach or exceed the exemption threshold—either the federal level or a lower state level—an annual gifting program can be a meaningful component of a longer-term tax reduction strategy.

There are also specific gift tax exclusions for certain types of transfers that don't count against either the annual exclusion or the lifetime exemption. Payments made directly to an educational institution for tuition—not room and board, not books, but tuition specifically—are excluded from gift tax entirely under what is called the educational exclusion. Payments made directly to a medical provider for healthcare expenses are similarly excluded. Grandparents who want to help fund a grandchild's education can make direct tuition payments to the institution in any amount, without those payments affecting their annual exclusion gifts or their lifetime exemption. This is one of the more powerful and underutilized gifting strategies available to older adults with larger estates.

529 educational savings plans add another dimension to education-focused giving. Contributions to a 529 plan for a beneficiary are treated as gifts to that beneficiary and count against the annual exclusion, but a special rule allows a contributor to front-load five years of annual exclusions into a single 529 contribution—up to $90,000 per beneficiary as of current limits—without triggering gift tax or using any lifetime

exemption, provided no further annual exclusion gifts are made to the same beneficiary during the five-year period.

## Putting the Numbers in Context

The purpose of working through these thresholds and mechanisms is not to turn you into a tax specialist. It is to help you answer one practical question with accuracy rather than anxiety: does my estate have meaningful tax exposure, and if so, where?

For most readers, the honest answer is that federal estate tax is not a concern at current exemption levels, state-level tax may or may not be relevant depending on your state of residence and the size of your estate, and the gift tax rules offer opportunities for tax-efficient giving rather than threats to routine generosity. For the smaller group of readers whose estates approach the relevant thresholds—whether federal or state—the answer is that professional guidance on specific strategies is worth the investment, and that the strategies available are well-established and effective when implemented deliberately.

Either way, clarity about your actual exposure is the foundation. Decisions made in response to a threat that doesn't exist waste resources that could protect against threats that do. And decisions postponed because the tax question seemed too complicated to understand leave real vulnerabilities unaddressed. The sections ahead address those vulnerabilities directly—moving from tax exposure into the specific tools available for protecting assets from creditors, from the costs of long-term care, and from the other risks that threaten what you've built.

## 5.2 Strategies That Actually Work — And the Person Each One Serves Best

Understanding your tax exposure is necessary. Knowing what to do about it is what makes that understanding useful. The strategies covered in this section are legitimate, well-established tools used by estate planning attorneys across the country. None of them require exotic offshore arrangements, aggressive tax shelters, or the kind of complexity that invites IRS scrutiny. What they require is deliberate planning, appropriate professional guidance, and an honest assessment of which approach fits your specific situation—because not every strategy serves every person equally well, and applying the wrong tool to the wrong circumstance can create more problems than it solves.

---

### Annual Gifting: The Simplest Tool for Gradual Estate Reduction

The annual gift tax exclusion, introduced in the previous section, is the most accessible estate reduction strategy available to anyone, regardless of estate size or sophistication. The ability to give up to $18,000 per year to any number of recipients—with no gift tax filing requirement, no reduction in lifetime exemption, and no restriction on how the recipient uses the money—creates a straightforward mechanism for moving wealth out of a taxable estate over time.

The math compounds meaningfully with consistency. A grandparent with four grandchildren who gives each one $18,000 annually removes $72,000 from their estate each year. Over ten years, that's $720,000 transferred to the next generation completely outside the estate tax system, assuming the current exclusion amount holds. A married couple doing the same thing through gift splitting removes $1.44 million from their combined estate over the same period.

Annual gifting works best for seniors who have estates large enough to benefit from reduction, whose cash flow is stable enough that removing assets doesn't create financial vulnerability, and who have identified specific individuals they want to benefit during their lifetime rather than at death. It is not a strategy that requires significant wealth to implement—but it delivers the most measurable tax benefit to estates that exceed or approach state-level exemption thresholds, where each dollar removed from the estate translates to a concrete reduction in eventual tax liability.

The limitation of annual gifting is its pace. It works gradually, through consistent application over many years, and it requires that the donor maintain enough assets for their own security throughout the process. A gifting program that leaves the donor financially dependent on their children's goodwill has traded one risk for another, and that trade is rarely worth making.

### Irrevocable Trusts: Removing Assets Permanently From the Taxable Estate

Where a revocable living trust keeps assets under the grantor's control and inside the taxable estate, an irrevocable trust does the opposite. Once assets are transferred into an irrevocable trust, the grantor relinquishes ownership and control of those assets. They no longer belong to the grantor's taxable estate for federal or state estate tax purposes. They are also generally protected from the grantor's future creditors, because the grantor no longer legally owns them.

This permanent transfer is both the source of the irrevocable trust's power and the reason it requires careful thought before implementation. Unlike a revocable trust, which can be amended, funded, or dissolved at will, an irrevocable trust cannot be undone without the consent of the beneficiaries and, in some cases, a court order. Whatever you put in is, for practical purposes, no longer yours to reclaim.

Several specific types of irrevocable trusts serve different planning purposes. An irrevocable life insurance trust, commonly abbreviated as an ILIT, holds a life insurance policy outside the taxable estate so that the policy's death benefit passes to heirs free of estate tax. Life insurance death benefits are included in the taxable estate if the deceased owned the policy at the time of death—a fact that surprises many people and creates unexpected tax liability in otherwise modest estates. Transferring an existing policy into an ILIT, or having the trust purchase a new policy, removes the death benefit from the estate entirely. The trust pays the premiums using annual exclusion gifts from the grantor, and the death benefit passes to the named beneficiaries outside of both probate and the taxable estate.

An irrevocable trust best serves seniors with larger estates who have identified assets they are confident they can permanently transfer without creating financial vulnerability, who want to provide for specific beneficiaries in a tax-efficient way, and who are working with an estate planning attorney experienced in trust administration. It is not a tool for everyone, and the decision to use one should never be made hastily or under external pressure.

## Spousal Lifetime Access Trusts: Tax Reduction Without Total Loss of Access

One of the most significant objections to irrevocable trust planning is the loss of access. Giving up control of assets permanently is a meaningful sacrifice, and for seniors whose financial security depends on retaining flexibility over their wealth, a fully irrevocable structure can feel like too large a concession to make in exchange for tax benefits that may or may not materialize.

The spousal lifetime access trust, known by its acronym SLAT, addresses this concern directly. A SLAT is an irrevocable trust created by one spouse for the benefit of the other. The grantor spouse transfers assets into the trust, removing them from the grantor's taxable estate, and the beneficiary spouse retains access to distributions from the trust during their lifetime. Because the beneficiary spouse can still access the assets, the family's overall financial security is maintained even though the grantor spouse has technically surrendered ownership.

The tax logic is straightforward: assets transferred to the SLAT are no longer part of the grantor spouse's taxable estate and are protected from the grantor's creditors. If the trust is properly structured, the assets may also be excluded from the beneficiary spouse's estate, depending on how the distribution terms are written and how state law treats the beneficial interest.

The SLAT strategy works best for married couples with estates large enough to benefit from reduction but with ongoing income needs that make a complete irrevocable transfer feel too restrictive. It requires that the marriage remain intact—a SLAT generally unravels in its practical benefit if the couple divorces, since the grantor spouse loses both the asset and access to it. It also requires careful structuring to avoid what tax attorneys call the reciprocal trust doctrine: if each spouse simultaneously creates a SLAT for the other with substantially identical terms, the IRS may treat the transfers as offsetting and pull both trusts back into the respective estates. A qualified attorney will structure any SLAT arrangement to avoid this outcome.

The profile of the senior for whom a SLAT makes the most sense is a married individual with a taxable estate, a need for ongoing financial flexibility, and a stable marital relationship. It is one of the more sophisticated tools in the estate planning toolkit, and it belongs in a conversation with a tax-focused estate attorney rather than in a do-it-yourself document.

---

**Beneficiary Designations as an Estate Planning Tool**

Beneficiary designations don't typically appear in lists of asset protection strategies, but they belong there. Assets that pass by beneficiary designation—retirement accounts, life insurance policies, annuities, and accounts with payable-on-death or transfer-on-death designations—pass entirely outside of probate and, importantly, outside of the testamentary estate governed by your will. They transfer directly to the named beneficiary at death, quickly and privately, without court involvement.

From an asset protection standpoint, beneficiary designations serve two functions worth understanding. First, they keep assets out of the probate estate, which means they are not accessible to creditors who file claims against the probate estate during the administration process. A life insurance death benefit paid directly to a named beneficiary is generally beyond the reach of the deceased's creditors. Second, they can be structured to provide inherited assets with a measure of protection from the beneficiary's own creditors, particularly when the beneficiary designation directs funds into a trust rather than to an individual outright.

Naming a trust as beneficiary of a retirement account requires particular care, because the tax treatment of inherited retirement accounts depends heavily on the beneficiary's classification under the tax code. The rules governing required minimum distributions for inherited IRAs changed significantly with the SECURE Act legislation, and naming a trust as IRA beneficiary can either preserve or complicate tax-deferred growth depending on how the trust is drafted. This is an area where the intersection of estate planning and tax planning requires coordinated professional advice rather than independent decisions made in each domain.

The senior for whom careful beneficiary designation work delivers the most value is one with significant assets in retirement accounts or life insurance, beneficiaries who might benefit from creditor protection or structured distributions, and an estate plan that hasn't been reviewed since any major legislative change affecting inherited account rules.

# Chapter 6 — Planning for Long-Term Care Costs

## 6.1 The Numbers Nobody Wants to Look At

There is a particular kind of financial denial that surrounds long-term care, and it is different in character from other planning blind spots. People who diligently fund retirement accounts, who review their investment portfolios quarterly, who spent weeks comparing Medicare supplement plans—these same people often carry an unexamined assumption that serious, sustained care needs won't happen to them, or that if they do, the cost will somehow be manageable without specific preparation. The assumption isn't born from carelessness. It comes from the same instinct that makes it difficult to write a will: confronting the scenario in detail feels like inviting it.

The problem is that long-term care costs don't become more manageable by remaining unexamined. They become more surprising, more disruptive, and more destructive to the financial security a family spent decades building. The numbers in this section are not presented to frighten anyone. They are presented because an accurate picture of what care actually costs is the only foundation on which a realistic plan can be built—and because the gap between what most people expect and what they will actually encounter is wide enough to swallow an estate.

---

**Why Long-Term Care Is Different From Other Retirement Expenses**

Retirement planning typically addresses a predictable range of ongoing expenses—housing, food, transportation, healthcare premiums and out-of-pocket costs, leisure, and the gradual inflation that erodes purchasing power over time. These expenses are estimable. They vary at the margins but follow recognizable patterns that financial planners have modeled for decades.

Long-term care doesn't follow that pattern. It is a contingent expense—one that may never materialize significantly, or that may arrive suddenly and with extraordinary force. The distribution of long-term care costs across the population is deeply unequal: many people die without ever needing sustained paid care, while others spend years in high-cost facilities that exhaust assets that took a lifetime to accumulate. The uncertainty is not about whether costs are high when they occur—they consistently are—but about whether and when they will occur for any given individual, and in what form.

This contingency is what makes long-term care financially dangerous in a way that other retirement expenses are not. You can save for predictable expenses incrementally over time. A contingent expense of potentially unlimited duration that might begin tomorrow or might never begin at all requires a different kind of preparation—one that most conventional retirement planning frameworks don't adequately address.

The other dimension that distinguishes long-term care from other retirement costs is its interaction with the rest of the estate plan. Long-term care expenses don't exist in isolation. They compete directly with the assets intended for a surviving spouse's financial security, for children's inheritances, and for charitable intentions. A prolonged nursing home stay doesn't just cost money—it restructures the entire financial picture that an estate plan was built around, often rendering documents and strategies developed without this scenario in mind partially or entirely obsolete.

## What Care Actually Costs: Home Care

For most people, the preference when care becomes necessary is to remain at home. This preference is near-universal across age groups and income levels, and the home care industry has grown substantially to serve it. The category of home care encompasses a wide range of services and corresponding costs, and understanding those distinctions is important for planning purposes because the difference between occasional assistance and around-the-clock care represents an enormous range of expenditure.

Home health aides provide personal care assistance—help with bathing, dressing, grooming, meal preparation, light housekeeping, and medication reminders. They do not provide skilled medical care, which is a different category of service covered differently by insurance. As of the most recent comprehensive industry survey data available at the time of writing, the national median cost for a home health aide runs approximately $27 to $30 per hour, though this figure varies significantly by geography. In high-cost metropolitan areas on the coasts, rates of $35 to $45 per hour are common. In lower-cost rural areas, rates may fall somewhat below the national median.

The hourly rate understates the actual cost when care needs are ongoing. A person who needs eight hours of daily home health aide assistance—a level of need that is common among those with moderate cognitive impairment or significant mobility limitations—is looking at a monthly cost in the range of $6,500 to $8,000 at median rates, before any additional costs for supplies, home modifications, or supplementary services. A person who needs around-the-clock care at home faces monthly costs that frequently exceed $15,000 to $20,000, depending on whether care is provided by a single aide working extended shifts or by multiple aides covering different hours.

Adult day services, which provide structured programming and supervision in a community setting during daytime hours, offer a less expensive alternative for individuals who can remain at home overnight with family support. The national median daily rate for adult day services runs approximately $80 to $100 per day, translating to roughly $1,700 to $2,200 per month for five-day-per-week attendance. These programs serve an important function in supporting family caregivers—who bear an enormous and often underacknowledged burden in the long-term care system—but they address a specific level of need and are not a substitute for residential care when needs intensify.

**Assisted Living: The Middle Ground Most Families Underestimate**

Assisted living facilities occupy the middle ground of the long-term care spectrum—providing housing, meals, personal care assistance, and social programming in a residential setting, without the round-the-clock skilled nursing care that a nursing home provides. For individuals who need more support than can be practically managed at home but who don't yet require the intensive medical monitoring of a skilled nursing facility, assisted living represents the most common transition.

The cost of assisted living surprises most families who haven't researched it specifically. The national median monthly cost for assisted living as of recent survey data stands at approximately $4,500 to $5,000 per month for a base-level private room and standard services package. That figure represents roughly $54,000 to $60,000 annually—and it is a baseline, not a ceiling.

The critical detail that median figures don't convey is the structure of assisted living pricing, which almost universally involves a base rate supplemented by additional charges for specific levels of care. The monthly base rate typically covers housing, meals, and a defined package of personal care assistance. When a resident requires more intensive assistance—additional help with bathing, continence care, medication management beyond basic reminders, or specialized programming for dementia—those services are added to the monthly bill at rates that can increase the total cost by $1,000 to $3,000 or more above the stated base.

Memory care units within assisted living facilities, which provide specialized programming and secure environments for individuals with Alzheimer's disease or other forms of dementia, carry a premium above standard assisted living rates. National median costs for memory care run approximately $5,500 to $7,000 per month, with significant regional variation. In major metropolitan markets, costs of $8,000 to $10,000 per month for memory care are not unusual.

Geographic variation across all assisted living categories is substantial enough to matter significantly for planning purposes. States in the Northeast and on the West Coast consistently report costs well above national medians. States in the South and Midwest tend to fall below median, though even in lower-cost regions, costs have risen meaningfully over the past decade and continue to increase faster than general inflation.

## Nursing Facilities: When Intensive Care Is Required

A skilled nursing facility—colloquially called a nursing home—provides the highest level of residential long-term care, including around-the-clock nursing supervision, skilled medical care, rehabilitation services, and support for individuals with complex medical needs or significant functional limitations. It is the most expensive category of long-term care and the one most likely to exhaust assets rapidly when a stay extends beyond several months.

The national median cost for a private room in a skilled nursing facility currently runs approximately $9,000 to $10,000 per month, or roughly $108,000 to $120,000 annually. Semi-private room rates are somewhat lower—typically $7,500 to $8,500 per month nationally—though the cost differential between private and semi-private is narrower than many people expect, and facility availability often determines which option is accessible more than personal preference does.

Again, these are national medians that mask enormous regional variation. In Alaska, Connecticut, Massachusetts, and New York, nursing home costs of $12,000 to $15,000 per month for a private room are not exceptional. In states with lower costs of living and lower healthcare labor costs, the same level of care may run closer to $6,000 to $7,500 per month. The specific cost environment in your state and your likely care market—the area where you live and where your family is located—is the number that matters for your planning, and it deserves research beyond the national figures cited here.

Duration of stay compounds the cost picture in a way that point-in-time numbers don't capture. The median length of a nursing home stay is often cited in terms of short-term rehabilitation stays—the weeks following a hip replacement or stroke that Medicare covers for a limited period under specific conditions. But for individuals who require long-term custodial nursing home care, the duration extends well beyond the short-term rehabilitation window. Stays of one to three years are common; stays of four years or longer are not rare, particularly for individuals with progressive neurological conditions. At $9,000 to $10,000 per month, a three-year stay represents $324,000 to $360,000 in cumulative costs—and a five-year stay approaches or exceeds $600,000 at current rates.

## What Medicare Actually Covers—and What It Doesn't

No discussion of long-term care costs is complete without addressing the most persistent and consequential misconception in this entire planning domain: the belief that Medicare covers long-term care.

Medicare does not cover long-term custodial care. This is not a policy nuance or a qualification buried in fine print—it is a fundamental structural feature of the program that has been true since Medicare's inception, and it affects virtually every family that confronts a serious long-term care need without preparation.

What Medicare does cover is a limited period of skilled nursing facility care following a qualifying hospital stay of at least three days, for the purpose of rehabilitation from a specific illness, injury, or condition. Coverage under this provision is time-limited and condition-specific: Medicare covers the full cost of a skilled nursing facility for the first twenty days, requires a substantial daily copayment from days twenty-one through one hundred, and covers nothing beyond one hundred days. Once Medicare's skilled nursing coverage ends—either because the hundred-day limit is reached or because the patient is no longer making measurable progress toward rehabilitation goals—the patient is responsible for the full daily cost of continued care.

The transition from Medicare-covered rehabilitation to self-pay or Medicaid-funded custodial care is one of the most financially significant and emotionally difficult moments a family can face, and it frequently arrives with less notice and less time for preparation than anyone expected. Understanding that this transition exists, and that it represents the beginning rather than the end of long-term care costs for many families, is essential context for the planning strategies discussed in the sections ahead.

The numbers in this section are not comfortable to sit with. They are not meant to be. They are meant to replace the vague, unexamined assumption that care costs are somehow manageable without preparation with an accurate picture of what preparation actually needs to address. That picture—however sobering—is the starting point for the strategies in the next sections, which exist precisely because these costs, while significant, are not beyond the reach of thoughtful planning done early enough to matter.

## 6.2 How to Pay for Care — Choosing Your Funding Strategy Before the Crisis Chooses for You

The cost figures from the previous section carry a specific kind of weight. They are large enough to be alarming, varied enough to resist easy generalizations, and uncertain enough in their timing and duration to defy the kind of precise projection that most financial planning relies on. This combination—high cost, unpredictable timing, unknown duration—is exactly what makes long-term care funding one of the most genuinely difficult planning problems in personal finance.

The difficulty is compounded by a timing trap that catches many families off guard. The best time to put long-term care funding in place is years before care is needed, when health is good enough to qualify for insurance, when assets are structured properly to support a Medicaid strategy if that becomes relevant, and when the full range of options is still available. By the time care need becomes visible on the horizon—when a diagnosis has been made, when cognitive changes are apparent, when a first serious fall has occurred—many of those options have already closed. Insurance becomes unavailable or unaffordable. Medicaid planning timelines are compressed. Decisions that could have been made deliberately over years must now be made urgently over days.

What follows is a clear-eyed comparison of the primary funding mechanisms available, including what each one does well, where each one falls short, and the timing considerations that determine whether a given option remains viable for your specific situation.

**Traditional Long-Term Care Insurance**

Traditional long-term care insurance operates on the same basic principle as other insurance products: you pay premiums over time in exchange for the insurer's commitment to cover a defined benefit if a qualifying need arises. A qualifying need is typically defined as the inability to perform a specified number of activities of daily living—bathing, dressing, toileting, transferring, continence, and eating—or a cognitive impairment requiring substantial supervision. When the trigger conditions are met, the policy pays a daily or monthly benefit toward the cost of qualifying care, up to a maximum benefit amount and for a benefit period specified in the policy.

The appeal of traditional long-term care insurance is straightforward: it transfers the financial risk of a catastrophic care need from your estate to an insurance company, preserving assets for a surviving spouse or heirs while providing a funded source for care costs. A well-designed policy can cover a substantial portion of assisted living or nursing home costs, allowing a family to access quality care without liquidating real estate or retirement accounts under pressure.

The practical challenges of traditional long-term care insurance, however, are significant enough that the product has retreated substantially from the market over the past two decades. Many of the major insurers who dominated this space in the 1990s and early 2000s have exited the market entirely, and those who remain have repriced policies significantly in response to two developments they underestimated in earlier pricing models: people are living longer and using benefits for longer than actuarial projections anticipated, and the low interest rate environment that persisted for years compressed the investment returns insurers counted on to fund future claims.

The result is a product that is more expensive than it was a generation ago, available from fewer carriers, and subject to premium increases on existing policies that have sometimes been substantial. Policyholders who purchased traditional long-term care insurance in the 1990s have in many cases faced cumulative premium increases that significantly altered the economics of their coverage—sometimes to the point where maintaining the policy became difficult on a fixed income.

For individuals who are currently in their late fifties or early sixties, in good health, and can afford premiums that may increase over time, traditional long-term care insurance remains a viable option worth evaluating. Policies purchased at younger ages carry lower initial premiums and, in some cases, better terms than those available to older applicants. The window for affordable, medically underwritten long-term care insurance typically begins to close meaningfully in the late sixties, and applicants with certain health conditions—diabetes, cardiovascular disease, cognitive concerns, mobility limitations—may find coverage unavailable regardless of age.

If traditional long-term care insurance is on your list to consider, the time to act is now rather than after the next medical event. The conversation with an independent insurance broker who represents multiple carriers, rather than a captive agent representing a single company, will give you the most complete picture of what's available and at what cost.

### Hybrid Life and Long-Term Care Policies

The hybrid policy—a product that combines life insurance or an annuity with a long-term care benefit rider—emerged in large part as a response to the objections most commonly raised against traditional long-term care insurance. The central objection was always the use-it-or-lose-it nature of the product: if you pay premiums for twenty years and never need care, the money is simply gone, with no return of premium and no death benefit. For people who resisted paying for a benefit they might never use, the pure insurance model felt like a poor bet.

A hybrid policy addresses this objection by guaranteeing that the premium invested in the product will benefit someone regardless of whether long-term care is ever needed. The typical structure involves a lump-sum or multi-year premium payment that funds a life insurance policy with a long-term care acceleration or extension rider. If long-term care is needed, the policy's death benefit is accelerated to pay for qualifying care costs, often with an extension benefit that continues payments beyond the face value of the policy if care needs are prolonged. If care is never needed, the full death benefit passes to named beneficiaries at death. If the policyholder changes their mind about the product, many hybrid policies offer a return-of-premium provision allowing the investment to be recovered after a specified period.

The profile of the person for whom a hybrid policy makes the most sense is someone with a lump sum of assets—proceeds from a property sale, an inherited IRA that has been distributed, a maturing CD, or a concentrated cash position—who wants to reposition those funds into something that provides long-term care protection while maintaining a residual benefit for heirs if care is never needed. The single-premium or limited-payment structure avoids the ongoing premium payment concern that makes traditional insurance feel financially precarious on a fixed income, and the guaranteed death benefit eliminates the use-it-or-lose-it objection entirely.

The tradeoffs are equally worth understanding. Hybrid policies are typically more expensive on a cost-per-dollar-of-benefit basis than traditional long-term care insurance, because the premium must fund both the insurance benefit and the investment component underlying the death benefit. The long-term care benefit available per dollar invested may be lower than what a comparable premium would purchase in a traditional policy. And the lump-sum entry point—often $50,000 to $100,000 or more for meaningful coverage—places these products out of reach for individuals who don't have accessible liquid assets to reposition.

**Health Savings Accounts**

A health savings account, or HSA, is a tax-advantaged savings vehicle available to individuals enrolled in a high-deductible health plan. Contributions are tax-deductible, growth within the account is tax-free, and withdrawals for qualified medical expenses are tax-free—creating a triple tax advantage that no other savings vehicle matches. Long-term care insurance premiums, up to age-based limits defined by the IRS, qualify as eligible HSA expenses, as do certain out-of-pocket long-term care costs.

The HSA's role in long-term care planning is most powerful when contributions are made consistently over working years and the account balance is allowed to compound without being depleted by current medical expenses. An individual who contributes the maximum annual amount to an HSA beginning in their fifties and invests the balance in growth-oriented funds within the account can accumulate a meaningful reserve specifically earmarked for healthcare and long-term care costs in later years. Unlike a flexible spending account, HSA balances roll over indefinitely without a use-it-or-lose-it annual deadline, making multi-decade accumulation strategies practical.

The limitation of the HSA as a standalone long-term care funding strategy is straightforward: it works best as a supplement to other planning rather than as a primary funding source for catastrophic care costs. Even a well-funded HSA carrying $100,000 or more in accumulated balance represents roughly one to two years of nursing home care at current median costs—meaningful protection against shorter care needs, but insufficient by itself against a prolonged stay. For individuals who have access to an HSA and are not yet drawing it down for current expenses, maximizing contributions and allowing the balance to grow represents a sensible component of a diversified long-term care funding approach.

## Medicaid Eligibility Planning: The Strategy of Last Resort and Long-Term Preparation

Medicaid is the joint federal-state program that serves as the primary payer for long-term custodial care in the United States for individuals who meet financial eligibility requirements. As discussed in Chapter 5, qualifying for Medicaid requires meeting asset limits that vary by state but are generally low—typically $2,000 in countable assets for a single applicant, though certain assets including a primary residence, one vehicle, and personal property are generally excluded from the countable asset calculation.

For married couples, Medicaid's community spouse resource allowance protects a portion of the couple's combined assets for the non-applying spouse—the community spouse—who remains at home. The federal minimum and maximum allowances for the community spouse are adjusted periodically, and states set their specific allowances within the federal range. As of current guidelines, the community spouse may retain assets up to approximately $148,000 in states using the federal maximum, though this figure varies and changes with annual adjustments. The community spouse is also protected by minimum monthly income allowances designed to prevent complete impoverishment.

Medicaid planning, as a long-term care funding strategy, involves structuring assets in advance of need—well outside the five-year look-back period—so that an applicant can qualify for benefits without spending down all available resources. The irrevocable Medicaid asset protection trust is the primary vehicle for this purpose: assets transferred into the trust more than five years before a Medicaid application are generally not counted against the applicant's resource limit, because the look-back period has expired. The trust preserves those assets for heirs while allowing the grantor to qualify for Medicaid coverage of care costs.

Medicaid planning is not appropriate for everyone, and it involves real tradeoffs. Assets transferred to a Medicaid asset protection trust are irrevocably removed from the grantor's control. The grantor cannot reclaim them, cannot use them for non-care purposes, and must genuinely relinquish ownership. For individuals with sufficient resources to self-fund care or purchase insurance, Medicaid planning may not be the highest priority. For those with modest estates that long-term care costs could devastate entirely, advance Medicaid planning may be the most realistic strategy available for preserving anything for a surviving spouse or heirs.

The five-year look-back period is the determinative timing constraint. Planning done today protects assets from Medicaid consideration five years from now. Planning done the week a nursing home placement becomes necessary protects nothing, and may create penalty periods that leave a family with neither assets nor coverage during the gap.

# Chapter 7 — Communicating Your Plan to Family

## 7.1 The Conversation That Makes the Documents Work

Spend enough time around estate planning attorneys and elder law specialists and a pattern becomes impossible to ignore. The cases that end in litigation, in family estrangement, in bitter disputes that outlast the grief that sparked them—these are rarely cases where the documents were wrong. They are cases where the family was surprised. Where an adult child learned for the first time, standing in a probate attorney's office two weeks after their parent's death, that the house had already been transferred into a trust, that their sibling had been named sole successor trustee, that a stepparent was the primary beneficiary of a life insurance policy no one knew existed. The legal framework was sound. The communication had never happened.

A well-constructed estate plan is, at its most fundamental level, a set of decisions you've made about your life, your values, and the people you love. Those decisions don't exist in a vacuum. They affect real people with real expectations, real assumptions, and real emotional investments in outcomes they may have been imagining for years without ever saying so out loud. When those people encounter your decisions for the first time through a legal document after you're gone, they are processing grief and financial reality simultaneously, without context, without the ability to ask you questions, and without the benefit of hearing the reasoning that made your choices make sense.

The family meeting—done thoughtfully, at the right time, with the right structure—closes that gap. It doesn't require you to justify every decision or to open your financial life to full disclosure. It requires something more modest and more valuable: enough transparency that the people who matter most understand the shape of your plan, know their roles within it, and have heard directly from you why you made the choices you made.

**Why Families Avoid This Conversation**

The reluctance to discuss estate plans with family is understandable and nearly universal. Money has always been a fraught topic in most families, layered with decades of dynamics about fairness, favoritism, sacrifice, and unspoken expectations. Adding death to that mix—because an estate plan conversation is, at some level, a conversation about dying—amplifies the discomfort to a point where many people find it easier to simply not have the conversation at all.

There is also a specific fear that naming tends to make real. Discussing the trust, the will, the powers of attorney can feel like announcing that decline is imminent, that the conversation itself is a concession to mortality. For people who are active, healthy, and nowhere near the scenarios their documents address, calling a family meeting to discuss what happens when they die can feel premature at best and morbid at worst.

What this reluctance misses is that the alternative—silence—doesn't protect anyone from the difficulty. It simply moves the difficulty to a moment when it will be harder to navigate, when you won't be present to provide context, when relationships are more fragile, and when the decisions that seemed reasonable in the abstract will be interpreted through the lens of loss and whatever assumptions your family was carrying without realizing it. The discomfort of a living conversation is modest compared to the damage that silence can do to a family that encounters your plan for the first time under those conditions.

### When to Have the Meeting

There is no single right moment for a family estate planning conversation, but there are better and worse windows. The best time is when your documents are finalized and current—after the trust is funded, the powers of attorney are executed, and the healthcare directives are in place—so that what you're sharing reflects your actual plan rather than an intention that hasn't been implemented yet. Sharing a plan that subsequently changes without notice creates its own confusion and occasionally its own resentments.

A natural trigger for the conversation is any significant life event that already brings the family together: a holiday gathering, a family reunion, a milestone birthday. These moments lower the activation energy for a conversation that might otherwise require special scheduling and therefore special psychological preparation. A family already assembled for Thanksgiving is not startled by a dinner table conversation shifting toward something important; a family summoned specifically for a meeting about estate planning may arrive already anxious about what they're about to hear.

Health events—a diagnosis, a surgery, a hospitalization—also commonly prompt this conversation, though they introduce an emotional urgency that can make the discussion harder to conduct calmly. If a health event is what finally motivates the meeting, the priority is honesty about what the documents say and who holds what authority, rather than detailed explanation of every planning decision. The most important information in a health-event context is practical: who is the healthcare agent, where are the documents, what does the living will say, who should be contacted.

Ideally, the conversation happens before any of these forcing events, while everyone—including you—is in a position to engage thoughtfully rather than reactively. The best version of this meeting is not urgent. It is deliberate.

**Who Should Be Present**

The question of who to include in a family estate planning conversation deserves more thought than it typically receives. The instinct is often to include everyone simultaneously—all the children, the spouses, perhaps older grandchildren—on the theory that information shared once with everyone present is information that can't be selectively reported or misremembered. That instinct has real merit in some situations and real drawbacks in others.

A meeting that includes all adult children and their spouses works well when relationships are functional, when the plan is relatively straightforward, and when there are no significant disparities between what different children will receive or what roles they've been assigned. It works less well when family dynamics include a history of conflict between siblings, when a blended family creates inherent tension between sets of children, or when you've made decisions—an unequal distribution, a single trustee when there are multiple children—that are likely to generate strong reactions.

In the latter situations, sequential individual conversations before any group meeting can be more effective. Speaking privately with the child you've named as sole successor trustee before announcing that decision in a room with their siblings allows you to explain your reasoning directly and gives that person time to process the responsibility before being observed doing so by their family. Speaking privately with a child who is receiving a smaller share—whether because of prior gifts, financial differences between siblings, or other reasons—allows you to have an honest conversation without the charged atmosphere of an audience.

Spouses and partners of your adult children present their own consideration. They are part of your family and part of the households that will be affected by your plan, which argues for their inclusion. They are not, however, your primary heirs or your appointed agents, and their presence in an estate planning conversation can sometimes shift the dynamic in ways that complicate the discussion—particularly if sibling relationships are already navigating in-law tensions. There is no universally correct answer, but it is worth deciding deliberately rather than defaulting to whoever happens to be present.

### Structuring the Conversation: Agenda and Tone

A family estate planning meeting doesn't need to be formal, but it benefits from structure. A conversation that begins without a clear purpose tends to drift into the topics that are easiest to discuss rather than the ones that are most important, and it tends to end without anyone being confident about what was actually communicated.

A useful structure covers four areas in sequence. First, the why: a brief explanation of why you're having this conversation now, framed not as a sign of decline but as an act of care for the people in the room. This framing matters because it sets the emotional register for everything that follows. You are not calling this meeting because you are dying. You are calling it because you have taken seriously your responsibility to the people you love, and you want them to be prepared rather than surprised.

Second, the what: an overview of the plan's structure without necessarily sharing every financial detail. Your family needs to know that a trust exists, that the trust governs how your assets will be distributed, that a pour-over will serves as the backstop, and that healthcare and financial powers of attorney are in place and with whom. They do not necessarily need to know the specific dollar values of every account, the precise terms of every distribution, or the details of every asset you own. The structure is the information that prevents chaos; the full financial inventory is information you can choose to share or not based on your own judgment about what's appropriate and necessary.

Third, the who: the specific appointments you've made and why. Who is the successor trustee, and what does that role involve. Who holds the financial power of attorney. Who is the healthcare agent and what authority do they have. Hearing these appointments directly from you—with whatever context you choose to provide about your reasoning—is fundamentally different from discovering them in a document. It transforms an assignment into a conversation. It gives the people in those roles the chance to ask questions and the chance to understand what you expect of them. It gives the people not in those roles the chance to hear your reasoning rather than constructing their own interpretation of it.

Fourth, the where: practical information about document location, key contacts, and what to do first in an emergency or at death. Who is the estate planning attorney. Where are the original documents. Where is the critical contacts summary discussed in Chapter 4. What accounts exist and at which institutions. This information is purely practical and carries no emotional charge—

but it is the information that will determine whether your plan can actually be administered efficiently when the time comes.

## What to Keep Private

Full disclosure is not the goal. The goal is sufficient transparency that the people responsible for carrying out your plan understand it, that the people affected by it aren't blindsided by it, and that the decisions you've made have been communicated in your own words rather than discovered through documents after you're gone.

The specific dollar values of your accounts, the terms of any charitable bequests you prefer to keep private, the details of any special needs planning for a family member, and any provisions designed to protect a beneficiary's inheritance from their creditors or a troubled marriage are all categories of information you may reasonably choose not to share in a family meeting. Privacy in these areas is not deception—it is a recognition that detailed financial disclosure to a group of people creates its own complications, and that the information required for your plan to function is not the same as full transparency about every financial decision you've ever made.

What should never be kept private, regardless of how uncomfortable the conversation might be, is the basic structure of appointments and the existence of any provisions that are likely to surprise or disappoint someone. An adult child who discovers they were not named as trustee or healthcare agent is better prepared to receive that information from you, with your explanation, than from an attorney's office after your death. A surprise that arrives with context and reasoning is not the same kind of wound as a surprise that arrives with no explanation at all.

The family meeting is not the end of communication about your estate plan. It is the beginning of an ongoing, low-intensity transparency that keeps the people around you informed as your plan evolves. Every time you make a significant change—a new trustee, a revised distribution, a new healthcare directive—the people affected deserve to know. Not through formal announcement, but through the kind of direct, honest conversation that the first meeting establishes as the norm rather than the exception.

Your estate plan is built on paper, executed through legal formalities, and administered through professional structures. But the plan actually works—in the human sense of working, in the sense of preserving relationships and honoring intentions and keeping families intact through the hardest transitions they face—through conversation. Everything in the documents is preparation for moments that words, spoken directly and honestly between people who love each other, can either redeem or make infinitely harder.

The documents create the structure. The conversation gives it meaning.

## 7.2 Navigating the Dynamics That Can Unravel Everything

Estate plans don't fail in courtrooms as often as they fail in kitchens—at holiday dinners, in whispered phone calls between siblings after a parent's death, in the accumulated weight of old grievances finding new expression through the language of fairness and inheritance. The legal documents are sound. The intentions were clear. But the human architecture surrounding those documents—the decades of family history, the unresolved tensions, the competing narratives about who sacrificed what and who was always favored—was never addressed directly, and now it has nowhere to go except into a dispute that costs everyone involved far more than any inheritance was worth.

Understanding the specific dynamics most likely to create this outcome, and having language ready for addressing them before they escalate, is not a soft addendum to estate planning. It is core planning work, and it deserves the same deliberate attention given to trust funding and tax strategy.

### Sibling Rivalry and the Perception of Fairness

Of all the dynamics that complicate estate planning conversations, the one that appears most consistently across family structures and income levels is the collision between equal and equitable. Most parents feel a powerful pull toward treating children equally in their estate plans—dividing assets in identical shares, appointing roles symmetrically, making no distinction that could be interpreted as favoritism. This impulse comes from a loving place. It also frequently produces outcomes that feel profoundly unfair to everyone involved.

Consider the family in which one adult child lived nearby and provided years of hands-on caregiving—managing medical appointments, coordinating household help, taking calls at all hours—while a sibling built a career in another city and visited three or four times a year. An equal division of the estate treats these two contributions as equivalent. The caregiving child, who may have foregone income and career advancement to be present, often experiences this as a significant injustice. The distant sibling, who may have contributed financially during that period, often genuinely doesn't understand why equal shares feel wrong to their sibling.

Neither position is dishonest. Both reflect real contributions and real costs that were never explicitly negotiated or acknowledged. The estate plan that ignores these realities in favor of mathematical equality doesn't resolve the underlying tension—it crystallizes it in legal form at the worst possible moment.

The communication strategy for this dynamic begins long before documents are signed. It involves naming what has happened directly: acknowledging the caregiving child's contribution explicitly, in conversation and ideally in the legacy letter discussed in the next section, whether or not the financial distribution reflects a differential. If you intend to provide a larger share to a caregiving child, say so—and say why—before the will is read rather than leaving the explanation to a document that arrives after your death. If you intend equal shares despite unequal contributions, acknowledge the inequality directly and explain the reasoning that led you there. What families cannot tolerate is not unequal treatment—it is unexplained treatment, which they will explain to themselves in the least charitable way available.

When raising this subject directly with the children involved, the language that tends to land best is language that acknowledges reality without assigning blame. Something in the register of: "I know the years of helping me have been harder on you than on your brother, and I want you to know I see that. Here's how I've tried to reflect it, and here's why I made the choices I made." This framing doesn't require a family meeting to become a negotiation or a grievance airing. It requires only that the person with the most information—you—share enough of it that the people left behind aren't left constructing the story themselves.

---

**Blended Families: When Love and Legal Structure Pull in Different Directions**

Blended families present the most structurally complex estate planning environment of any family configuration, and they present the most emotionally volatile communication challenges to match. The central tension is almost always some version of the same conflict: a surviving spouse's need for financial security and control pulls against biological children's expectation of inheriting their parent's share of the estate, and the legal structure of the estate plan determines which side of that tension prevails.

This tension doesn't require anyone to be villainous. A surviving spouse who controls inherited assets and redirects them—deliberately or simply through the passage of time and changing circumstances—toward their own biological children is acting on exactly the loyalties you would expect. Biological children who resent a stepparent's control over assets their deceased parent accumulated before the marriage are also acting on predictable and understandable loyalties. The conflict is structural, not personal, and it plays out with remarkable consistency across blended families regardless of the wealth involved.

The communication work in blended families happens on two tracks simultaneously. The first track involves the surviving spouse and the biological children of the deceased, and the message that needs to be delivered—clearly, directly, and before death makes direct delivery impossible—is that the estate plan has anticipated this tension and addressed it deliberately. If a qualified terminable interest property trust or a similar structure ensures that assets ultimately pass to biological children after the surviving spouse's death, the children need to know this. If the plan instead prioritizes the surviving spouse's financial security in ways that may reduce what children eventually receive, the children need to hear that directly and understand the reasoning, rather than discovering it when the surviving spouse's estate is eventually settled.

The second track involves the relationship between the person doing the planning and their current spouse, and it requires a frankness that many couples find uncomfortable. A conversation that acknowledges "I want to make sure you're financially secure, and I also want to make sure my children receive what I've always intended for them" is not a romantic conversation. It is a necessary one. The estate plan that emerges from that conversation—whatever structure it takes—will be more durable and less contested than one drafted without the underlying tension having been named.

When raising this directly with a spouse, the framing that tends to be most productive is one that separates security from control. Most surviving spouses don't need unlimited control over all inherited assets to feel financially secure—they need reliable income, a stable home, and protection from the kind of financial pressure that makes everyday life anxious. A trust structure that provides those things while protecting the eventual inheritance of biological children addresses both needs without requiring either party to sacrifice what matters most to them. Presenting the plan in those terms—what it provides rather than what it restricts—changes the emotional register of the conversation significantly.

---

## Estranged Children and the Decisions Nobody Wants to Make

Perhaps the most personally painful communication challenge in estate planning involves estranged family members—children from whom a parent has been separated for years, either through the child's choices, the parent's choices, or the accumulated damage of circumstances that didn't resolve. The question of what to leave an estranged child, and how to document that decision in a way that reduces the likelihood of a legal challenge, sits at the intersection of legal planning and deeply personal history.

Completely disinheriting a child is legal in virtually every state for parents—unlike spouses, children have no automatic legal right to inherit under most state laws. But a will or trust that simply omits a child without explanation creates a vulnerability: a court may consider whether the omission was intentional or whether the child was accidentally overlooked, and an estranged child with legal standing to challenge the document may use that ambiguity as the basis for a contest.

The legal protection against this challenge is an explicit acknowledgment in the document—not a detailed explanation of the estrangement, but a clear statement that the omission is intentional and not an oversight. Language to the effect of "I have intentionally made no provision for my child [name] in this trust" gives a court little room to infer accident. Combined with a no-contest clause that penalizes unsuccessful challenges, this approach significantly reduces the legal vulnerability created by an intentional disinheritance.

The communication question—whether to contact an estranged child about this decision, and if so, how—has no universal answer. Some parents find that the estate planning process prompts a genuine reconsideration of whether an estrangement they've lived with for years still reflects their current feelings. Others feel certain that their decision is right but recognize that a brief direct communication prevents the discovery of that decision from being the additional wound of a post-death surprise. Still others conclude that contact would do more harm than good. These are decisions that belong to the individual making them, informed by the specific history involved, and no framework in a book can make them for you.

What the communication can include, when it happens, is a clear statement that requires no response and invites no negotiation: "I want you to know that I've completed my estate planning, and I've made the decision not to include you in my trust. I've made that decision deliberately, and I wanted you to hear it from me rather than discover it later." This is not a warm communication. It is an honest one, and it eliminates the possibility that the discovery happens in a courtroom instead.

# Chapter 8 — Keeping Your Plan Current for Life

## 8.1 When Your Plan Needs to Change — Recognizing the Triggers Before They Become Problems

There is a particular satisfaction that comes with completing an estate plan. The documents are signed, the trust is funded, the powers of attorney are executed, the healthcare directives are filed with the right people. For weeks or months, perhaps years, you've been meaning to get this done, and now it is done. The relief is real, and it is deserved. You have accomplished something that the majority of adults in this country never complete, and you have protected your family in ways that will matter enormously when the moments that test those protections actually arrive.

The temptation that follows that satisfaction is to treat the plan as finished—to file the documents, note the attorney's contact information somewhere accessible, and return to the rest of your life with the comfortable sense that this particular responsibility has been permanently discharged.

It hasn't. Not because the work was inadequate, but because the life the plan was built around will continue to change in ways that the documents cannot anticipate, and a plan that doesn't change with it will gradually diverge from the reality it was designed to govern. The divergence is rarely dramatic at first. A beneficiary who moves to another state. An account that was opened and never transferred to the trust. A tax law that adjusts a threshold.

A family relationship that shifted. Individually, each of these gaps is manageable. Collectively, accumulated over years without review, they can transform a carefully constructed plan into a document that no longer reflects who you are, what you own, or who you trust to carry out your wishes.

An estate plan is not a one-time project. It is a system that requires periodic maintenance and immediate response to specific triggering events—circumstances that change the underlying reality of your life significantly enough that the documents built on that reality need to be revisited before the gap between plan and reality widens into a problem.

**Marriage: Yours or a Beneficiary's**

Your own marriage or remarriage is among the most significant triggers for an immediate estate plan review, and it operates on multiple levels simultaneously. A new spouse creates new legal rights that vary by state but that can affect the distribution of your estate even if your existing documents don't acknowledge the marriage. In many states, a surviving spouse has statutory rights to a minimum share of an estate—called an elective share or forced share—that exist independently of what any will or trust provides. A plan built entirely around children from a prior relationship, without addressing a new spouse's legal position, may be contested or partially overridden by state law in ways that produce outcomes you didn't intend.

Beyond the legal mechanics, a new marriage changes the human architecture of your plan in ways that the documents need to reflect. The successor trustee you named before remarriage may or may not be the right choice in the context of your new family structure. The beneficiary designations on retirement accounts and life insurance policies—which pass entirely outside the trust—need to be reviewed to ensure they align with your current intentions rather than a prior chapter of your life. The healthcare agent you designated may be someone whose role in your life has changed.

When a child or grandchild marries, the review trigger operates differently but is equally important. A beneficiary's marriage introduces a new person into the equation who, in the event of a divorce, may have legal claims against assets your beneficiary has inherited depending on how those assets are managed and commingled. If your trust distributes a child's inheritance outright without any protective trust structure, those assets are potentially vulnerable to a future divorce settlement. The addition of a spendthrift clause, or the restructuring of a beneficiary's share into a continuing trust rather than an outright distribution, can provide meaningful protection that an outright inheritance does not. A child's marriage is the right moment to assess whether your current distribution terms still make sense given the new circumstances.

**Divorce: Yours or a Beneficiary's**

Divorce triggers one of the most urgent estate plan reviews of any life event, and the urgency applies both to your own divorce and to a beneficiary's.

Your own divorce—or legal separation—requires immediate action on multiple fronts. Most states have automatic revocation statutes that nullify provisions in favor of a former spouse in a will upon divorce, but these statutes do not uniformly apply to trusts, and they almost never apply automatically to beneficiary designations on retirement accounts and life insurance policies. A person who divorces and dies without updating their IRA beneficiary designation may inadvertently leave their retirement account to an ex-spouse, regardless of what the trust or will says, because the beneficiary designation controls and it hasn't been changed. This is not a theoretical risk—it is a documented pattern that appears in estate litigation with dismaying regularity.

The immediate steps following a divorce include reviewing and updating every beneficiary designation on every account, reassessing the trustee and agent appointments throughout your documents, and working with your estate planning attorney to determine whether your existing trust needs to be amended or whether a new document would better serve your post-divorce situation. If your former spouse held any role in your plan—as successor trustee, as executor, as financial or healthcare agent—those appointments need to be changed immediately, not after the dust settles.

A beneficiary's divorce signals a different kind of review. If you have a child going through a divorce, this is the moment to assess whether assets they will inherit from you are structured in a way that provides adequate protection from the divorce proceeding. It is also the moment to ensure that any grandchildren's interests are protected within your plan regardless of how the divorce ultimately resolves their parents' financial relationship.

---

### Death of a Beneficiary or Appointed Agent

The death of someone named in your estate plan—whether as a beneficiary, a successor trustee, an executor, or a healthcare agent—requires prompt review of the documents that include them. The urgency varies depending on the role.

The death of a primary successor trustee or healthcare agent is the most immediately significant, because it removes the person designated to step into your affairs during incapacity or at death.

If you named only a primary trustee and no alternate, or if both your primary and alternate have predeceased you, your trust has no designated successor and a court appointment may be necessary—exactly the outcome the trust was designed to avoid. The same logic applies to every appointed role in your plan. The depth of your backup designations—the alternates and the alternates to the alternates—determines whether your plan can continue functioning when the people originally named are no longer available.

The death of a beneficiary requires review of what your documents provide when a named beneficiary predeceases you. If the trust includes per stirpes distribution language, that beneficiary's share passes to their own descendants—a result you may or may not intend depending on your relationship with those descendants and their circumstances. If the trust instead provides that a predeceased beneficiary's share falls into the residue to be distributed among surviving beneficiaries, the reallocation may or may not reflect your current wishes. Neither outcome is automatically wrong, but both deserve conscious review rather than passive acceptance of whatever the document happens to say.

### Major Asset Acquisitions and Dispositions

Every significant change in your asset picture—a real estate purchase, an inheritance, the sale of a business, the receipt of a large settlement, the opening of a new investment account—is a trigger for reviewing whether the new asset is properly integrated into your trust.

The funding gap discussed in Chapter 2 doesn't close itself. Assets acquired after your trust is established don't automatically transfer into it. A vacation property purchased five years after your trust was funded is titled in your personal name unless you specifically took steps to deed it into the trust. An inherited brokerage account is in your name unless you specifically retitled it. These assets, if not addressed, will pass through your probate estate rather than through your trust—reintroducing exactly the delays, costs, and public exposure that the trust was built to avoid.

The practical discipline is simple in principle: every time you acquire a significant asset, ask immediately whether it belongs in the trust, and if so, complete the transfer before the question gets buried under the next set of priorities. For real estate, this means preparing and recording a new deed. For financial accounts, it means contacting the institution and completing whatever retitling process they require. For accounts with beneficiary designations, it means reviewing whether the designation is consistent with your overall plan or whether it creates an unintended inconsistency.

The sale of a major asset is equally worth noting, not because it creates a gap to fill, but because it may change the overall character of your estate in ways that affect your planning strategy. The sale of a business or a primary residence may produce a significant liquidity event that changes your estate's relationship to tax thresholds, that creates planning opportunities for gifting or charitable giving, or that simply requires updating the inventory of what the trust owns and what it's worth.

**Tax Law Changes**

Federal and state tax law governing estates, gifts, and inherited assets changes more frequently than most people realize, and the changes are not always announced in ways that reach people who aren't actively monitoring them. The sunset provision for the current elevated federal estate tax exemption—discussed in

Chapter 5—is one prominent example of a scheduled change with significant planning implications for estates that currently sit between the post-sunset threshold and the current one. The SECURE Act's changes to inherited retirement account rules, which altered the required distribution timeline for most non-spouse beneficiaries, is another example of legislation that required immediate review of trust provisions involving retirement accounts as beneficiaries.

A tax law change is a trigger for a professional review, not necessarily for wholesale revision of your documents. In many cases, the law changes in ways that don't affect your specific situation. But you cannot know whether a change affects you without understanding what changed and how it interacts with your plan's specific provisions. Maintaining a relationship with your estate planning attorney—even if contact is infrequent—ensures you have someone who can assess new developments in the context of your specific documents rather than relying on general news coverage that rarely provides the granular analysis a plan review requires.

**Relocation to a New State**

Moving from one state to another is a trigger that surprises many people, because the estate plan they built so carefully in one state may not translate seamlessly into another state's legal environment.

State laws governing trust administration, will execution requirements, powers of attorney, healthcare directives, community property rights, and state estate taxes vary meaningfully across jurisdictions. A healthcare directive executed in Florida may or may not be recognized by medical providers in Oregon without amendment. A power of attorney drafted under California law may encounter resistance from financial institutions in Texas that are accustomed to their own state's statutory form. A state estate tax in your new state of residence—if you've moved from a state without one to Massachusetts or Oregon or Washington—may create tax exposure that didn't exist before the move.

Relocation is the trigger for a state-specific review with an estate planning attorney licensed in your new state of residence. In most cases, your existing documents remain legally valid and can be updated with relatively modest amendments. In some cases—particularly when moving to or from a community property state, or to a state with a significantly different statutory framework for powers of attorney and healthcare directives—more substantial revision is appropriate. The cost of this review is modest. The cost of discovering that your documents don't work in your new state at the moment they need to is not.

The estate plan that was right for your life five years ago was built on the circumstances of five years ago. The one that will protect your family going forward needs to reflect the circumstances of today—and the discipline of reviewing it when your life sends the signals that review is warranted is the habit that keeps everything else working.

## 8.2 The Annual Review — One Hour a Year That Protects Everything Else

Most of the damage that accumulates in an estate plan between its creation and its administration doesn't happen in a single dramatic moment. It happens gradually, through the quiet accumulation of small gaps: a beneficiary designation that wasn't updated after a divorce, an account opened and never transferred to the trust, a successor trustee who moved across the country three years ago and hasn't been replaced, a healthcare directive sitting in a filing cabinet whose location only one person knew and that person has since died. None of these gaps announced themselves as problems when they formed. They simply waited, invisible and unaddressed, until the moment the plan needed to work and found itself unable to.

The annual review exists to find these gaps while they're still easy to close, before the circumstances that created them have been forgotten, and long before the event that would expose them as failures. It is not a comprehensive legal overhaul. It is not an occasion for reconsidering every decision in every document. It is a structured, systematic check of the specific elements most likely to drift out of alignment with reality over time, conducted with enough regularity that no single year's worth of drift becomes unmanageable.

Done properly, this review takes under an hour. Done consistently, it is the single most protective habit available to someone who has already built a solid estate plan.

## Choosing a Review Date and Making It Stick

The annual review works best when it's anchored to a fixed date that recurs naturally rather than requiring a decision each year about when to schedule it. Tax season is a popular choice because financial documents are already being gathered and reviewed, making it a natural moment to extend attention to the estate plan. A birthday is another option—particularly a milestone birthday—because it connects the review to a personal marker that's easy to remember. The anniversary of the trust's execution works for people who find meaning in that kind of continuity.

The specific date matters less than its consistency. A review that happens every January regardless of circumstances builds a habit that persists through busy years and distracted ones. A review that is supposed to happen "sometime in the spring when things slow down" tends to happen irregularly if at all. Pick a date, put it in whatever calendar system actually governs your life, and treat it with the same seriousness as a medical appointment—because in the context of your family's financial health, that's essentially what it is.

### Reviewing Beneficiary Designations

Beneficiary designations are the element of an estate plan most likely to be out of date, because they exist on individual accounts rather than in a centralized document, and because updating them requires a separate action with each financial institution rather than a single amendment to a single document. The result is that designations updated diligently on some accounts remain unchanged on others for years or decades.

The annual review begins by pulling the current beneficiary designation on file for every account that has one: retirement accounts including IRAs, 401(k)s, and 403(b)s; life insurance policies; annuities; and any bank or investment accounts with payable-on-death or transfer-on-death designations. Most financial institutions allow you to view current designations online or will provide them upon written request.

For each account, the review asks four questions. First, is the primary beneficiary still the right person—alive, in a relationship with you that reflects your current intentions, and in circumstances where an outright inheritance serves them well? Second, is the contingent beneficiary designation still appropriate, accounting for any deaths, divorces, or changed relationships since the designation was last updated? Third, does the designation coordinate properly with your trust—directing assets toward the trust where that's intended, or to individuals directly where that's more appropriate given the account type? Fourth, for retirement accounts specifically, is the designated beneficiary structured to take advantage of available stretch provisions under current tax law, or has the designation been rendered suboptimal by changes in the rules governing inherited accounts?

Any designation that can't be answered satisfactorily to all four questions gets flagged for follow-up with the relevant institution before the review is considered complete.

**Verifying Trustee and Agent Readiness**

The people named in your documents are not static. They age, they relocate, their health changes, their relationships with you evolve, and their circumstances shift in ways that affect their ability and willingness to serve in the roles you've assigned them. A successor trustee who seemed like the obvious choice four years ago may have developed health problems of their own, may be managing a demanding career transition, or may have moved to a time zone that makes prompt response to emergencies genuinely difficult.

The annual review includes a direct check—not necessarily a formal conversation every year, but at minimum a current assessment—of whether each person named in your documents remains the right person for their role and whether they remain willing and able to serve. This is particularly important for successor trustees and healthcare agents, whose roles require prompt action under stressful circumstances, but it applies equally to alternate appointments that exist precisely for moments when primary designees are unavailable.

If the review surfaces a concern about any appointment—a named trustee whose circumstances have changed significantly, an alternate executor you've lost touch with, a healthcare agent whose values no longer feel aligned with yours—the appropriate response is an amendment to the relevant document, not a mental note to deal with it later. Amendments are typically straightforward documents that your estate planning attorney can prepare at modest cost, and they are infinitely easier to execute while you're healthy and thinking clearly than under the urgency of a health event.

### Checking Account Titling and Trust Funding

The trust funding audit is the component of the annual review most likely to surface a concrete, actionable gap. It involves comparing a current list of your significant assets against the trust's ownership of those assets, identifying any property that should be in the trust but isn't, and completing the transfers needed to close the gap.

Begin by listing every significant asset you own: real property, bank accounts, investment and brokerage accounts, business interests, valuable personal property, and any other assets that represent meaningful value. For each item on the list, verify the current title or ownership designation. Real estate ownership can be verified through county property records, which are generally accessible online through the county assessor or recorder's office. Bank and investment account titling can be verified through account statements or by contacting the institution directly.

Any asset that should be in the trust based on your original funding decisions but that appears in your individual name rather than the trust's name is a gap that needs to be closed. This might be a new account opened since the trust was established, a vehicle or piece of property acquired and never transferred, or an asset whose title reverted to your personal name during a transaction—a refinancing, for example, sometimes results in a property being temporarily deeded out of a trust and never deeded back in.

The practical steps for closing these gaps are the same ones covered in Chapter 2: a new deed recorded with the county for real estate, a retitling request submitted to the financial institution for accounts, a general assignment for tangible personal property that doesn't have a formal title. None of these steps is complex, but all of them require follow-through rather than good intentions, and the annual review is the mechanism that ensures follow-through actually happens.

### Confirming Document Storage and Accessibility

The final element of the annual review verifies that the people who need to access your documents in an emergency can actually do so—that the critical contacts summary is current, that document locations haven't changed without being communicated, and that the people holding copies of key documents still have those copies and know where they are.

This check takes ten minutes and is almost always skipped. Don't skip it. The successor trustee whose copy of the trust was in an email attachment on a laptop they replaced two years ago and never transferred is not meaningfully better positioned than a trustee who never had a copy at all. The healthcare agent who thinks your living will is in the filing cabinet in the spare bedroom doesn't know that you moved it to the home safe when you changed the house locks last spring.

Review the critical contacts summary, update any information that has changed—attorney, accountant, financial advisor, insurance agent, physician—and confirm that the people who need this information have the current version. If you've made any document changes during the year, ensure that everyone holding copies has been given the updated versions and that superseded documents have been clearly marked as revoked rather than left in circulation as potential sources of confusion.

# Conclusion: Your Family's Future Starts Today

## 9.1 The Arc of a Complete Plan — From Understanding to Action

Margaret's story opened this book. She was 71, sharp and capable, with a mental list of things she'd get to when life slowed down. The estate plan was on that list. It stayed there until a Tuesday morning in February made it irrelevant—not because she ran out of time to care, but because she ran out of time to act. What followed consumed seventeen months, $23,000, and the functional relationships between three adult children who had loved each other before a probate court became the arena for their grief.

That story was the starting point. Everything in the eight chapters that followed was the answer to it—not a theoretical answer, but a practical one, built from the specific tools and decisions that would have changed the outcome entirely had Margaret used them. You now have those tools. What remains is understanding how they fit together as a single coherent system rather than a collection of independent documents, and committing to the action that transforms understanding into protection.

### The Foundation: Knowing What You're Working With

The journey began with clarity about the three pillars that govern every estate: wills, trusts, and probate. Chapter 1 established the distinction that most people never learn until it's too late—that a will is not an alternative to probate but a set of instructions addressed to it, and that the probate process it triggers is slower, more expensive, more public, and more disruptive to families than the quiet, private transfer that a properly funded trust provides. The side-by-side comparison between a will and a revocable living trust dismantled the most persistent myth in estate planning: that trusts are instruments of the wealthy, beyond the reach and relevance of ordinary families who own a home, carry a retirement account, and love people they want to protect.

What emerged from that first chapter was a framework for honest self-assessment—an understanding of where each reader stands relative to the tools available, whether single, married, widowed, or navigating the particular complexity of a blended family. That framework was not academic. It was the diagnostic that determined which documents belonged in each person's plan and why.

**The Core Structure: Trust, Will, and the Documents Between Them**

Chapters 2 and 3 built the central architecture. The revocable living trust—its grantors, trustees, successor trustees, and beneficiaries—came into focus not as a legal abstraction but as a human structure populated by real people making consequential choices about who they trust, what they're trying to protect, and how they want their assets to reach the people they love. The drafting process, the distribution decisions, the provisions for minor grandchildren and beneficiaries with disabilities, the clauses that should never be omitted—all of it translated into practical guidance that a reader could carry into an attorney's office with genuine understanding of what they were building and why.

Funding—the critical step that most plans skip or complete only partially—received the emphasis it deserves, because a trust that isn't funded is a shell that provides none of the protection it was designed to deliver. Real estate, financial accounts, personal property, retirement accounts: each category has its own transfer mechanics, and the discipline of keeping the funding current as life continues to bring new assets is the habit that keeps the trust effective rather than merely existing.

Chapter 3 completed the document structure with the pour-over will—the safety net that catches everything the trust missed—and addressed the legal formalities, executor selection, specific bequests, and guardianship nominations that make a will functional rather than merely present. The two documents together, trust and pour-over will, form the foundation of a plan that governs the entire estate rather than just the portion its creator remembered to address explicitly.

## Incapacity: The Planning Dimension Nobody Discusses Enough

Chapter 4 shifted the frame from death to incapacity—the scenario that affects more families, arrives with less warning, and receives less planning attention than any other dimension of estate planning. The durable financial power of attorney and the healthcare directive are not supporting documents subordinate to the trust. They are essential instruments that address a category of risk the trust cannot touch: the period when you are still alive but unable to make or communicate decisions about your own finances and healthcare.

The alternative to these documents is a court-supervised conservatorship for financial matters and a family in crisis making medical decisions without guidance for healthcare matters. Neither alternative is acceptable once you understand it clearly, and the chapter made both the alternatives and the protections concrete enough that the decision to act became obvious rather than optional. The practical guidance on choosing agents, setting appropriate limits on their authority, and ensuring documents are accessible when they're needed—culminating in the critical contacts summary—transformed the legal framework into a system that actually functions under real emergency conditions.

---

**Protection: Taxes, Creditors, and the Cost of Care**

Chapters 5 and 6 addressed the two financial threats most likely to erode what an estate plan is meant to preserve: tax exposure and long-term care costs.

The tax chapter began with the demystification that most people need before they can think clearly about this subject—an honest accounting of who the federal estate tax actually affects, what the relevant thresholds are, where state-level taxes create exposure that the federal picture doesn't, and how the gift tax rules offer planning opportunities rather than just threats. From that accurate foundation, the legitimate protection strategies—annual gifting, irrevocable trusts, spousal lifetime access trusts, careful beneficiary designation work—became tools calibrated to actual situations rather than solutions in search of problems. The firm line between legitimate planning and fraud, and the specific warnings about Medicaid look-back periods and the scams that target seniors, ensured that the protection strategies discussed were the ones that actually protect rather than the ones that create new vulnerabilities.

The long-term care chapter confronted the numbers that most people prefer to avoid—the actual median costs of home care, assisted living, and skilled nursing facilities, and the duration of stays that translate those monthly figures into the total financial impact on a family. Medicare's fundamental limitation as a long-term care payer was stated plainly, because the misconception that Medicare covers custodial care is too consequential to leave unaddressed. The funding strategies—traditional long-term care insurance, hybrid policies, health savings accounts, Medicaid eligibility planning—were compared with attention to timing, because the window during which each option remains available is the constraint that makes early action essential rather than merely advisable. The integration of these funding mechanisms with the trust structure showed how a coherent strategy addresses multiple risks simultaneously rather than treating each threat in isolation.

### Communication: The Human Work That Makes Legal Work Matter

Chapter 7 addressed the dimension of estate planning that no document can substitute for: the human conversations that determine whether a plan actually functions as intended when the people it affects encounter it. The family meeting—its timing, its agenda, its careful calibration of what to share and what to keep private—is not a courtesy extended to heirs. It is a structural component of the plan, because a plan discovered rather than communicated is a plan that arrives without context at the worst possible moment.

The specific dynamics most likely to derail plans—sibling rivalry rooted in equal versus equitable treatment, blended family tensions between spousal security and biological children's expectations, the legally and emotionally complex territory of estranged children—received the direct treatment they deserve, with language that acknowledges reality honestly rather than pretending that careful legal drafting resolves tensions that are fundamentally human in character.

The legacy letter closed the chapter by addressing what no legal document can convey: the reasoning behind the decisions, the values that shaped a life, the hopes carried forward to the people who will carry the name and the memory. It transforms the estate plan from a financial instrument into a personal statement—not by replacing the legal structure but by giving it the meaning that legal language cannot supply. Together, the document and the letter accomplish what neither could alone: they transfer both the assets and the understanding of why those assets matter and where they came from.

**Maintenance: The Habit That Protects Everything Else**

Chapter 8 completed the arc by establishing that an estate plan is not a project with a finish line but a system with a maintenance requirement. The trigger events that demand immediate review—marriage, divorce, death of a named party, major asset changes, tax law amendments, relocation—are not rare disruptions to a stable plan. They are the normal events of a continuing life, and a plan that doesn't respond to them gradually diverges from the reality it was built to govern until the gap becomes a problem no one anticipated.

The annual review—an hour, a fixed date, a consistent structure—is the mechanism that closes that gap before it widens. The distinction between what can be maintained independently and what requires professional involvement is the judgment that ensures professional time is invested where it genuinely matters rather than either avoided entirely or applied indiscriminately to questions that don't require it.

### What the Eight Chapters Add Up To

Taken individually, each chapter addresses a component. Taken together, they describe a complete system: understand the tools, build the structure, address incapacity, manage financial risk, protect against care costs, communicate with the people who matter, and maintain the plan as life continues to change. Each element supports the others. A trust without a pour-over will has a gap. A trust without funded accounts is a shell. Documents without communication are surprises waiting to happen. Communication without maintenance becomes outdated. The system works because all of its parts work together, and it requires attention because any part left unattended weakens the whole.

Margaret didn't need a law degree to have protected her family. She needed the understanding that this book has provided and the decision to act on it before Tuesday morning in February made action impossible. You have the understanding. The decision that remains is yours.

## 9.2 The Next Seven Days — Three Tasks That Change Everything

There is a particular kind of reader who finishes a book like this one, sets it down with genuine conviction, and does nothing. Not because the conviction wasn't real. Not because the information wasn't useful. But because the distance between understanding and action is wider than it appears, and without a specific next step attached to a specific timeline, the energy that built during reading dissipates into the general pressure of ordinary life. The estate plan stays on the mental list, right where it has always been, waiting for a moment of lower urgency that never quite arrives.

This section exists to close that distance. Not with a comprehensive project plan that requires weeks of preparation before anything can begin, but with three specific tasks that can be completed within the next seven days regardless of where you currently stand in the process. These tasks don't finish your estate plan. They start it in a way that creates momentum, and momentum—in estate planning as in most things that matter—is more valuable than a perfect strategy that never leaves the page.

---

**Task One: Gather Your Key Documents**

Before any attorney can help you build or update an estate plan, and before you can make informed decisions about the components that plan requires, you need an accurate picture of what you currently have. This first task is purely organizational, requires no professional assistance, and can be completed in a single focused sitting of one to two hours.

Gather every document that touches your financial and legal life: existing wills, any trust documents already in place, deeds to real property, titles to vehicles, life insurance policies with their current beneficiary designations, retirement account statements, bank and investment account statements, any powers of attorney or healthcare directives that have been previously executed, Social Security statements, pension documentation, and any business ownership agreements if applicable.

As you gather these documents, make a simple written inventory—not a formal legal document, just a list on paper or a computer document—that records what you have, where the original is stored, and in the case of financial accounts, which institution holds each one. This inventory serves two purposes simultaneously. It gives your estate planning attorney the information they need to assess your situation accurately and efficiently in the initial consultation, which saves professional time and therefore professional fees. And it gives the people who will administer your estate eventually—your successor trustee, your executor, whoever steps into those roles when the time comes—the roadmap they will desperately need and that most estates don't provide.

If this document gathering surfaces an existing will or trust that was executed years ago and hasn't been reviewed since, read through it. Not to evaluate its legal adequacy—that's the attorney's job—but to assess whether the people named in it still make sense, whether the assets it references still exist in the form described, and whether the distribution terms still reflect your intentions. Surprises discovered now, in the quiet of your own home, are infinitely easier to address than surprises discovered in an administrative crisis after your death.

**Task Two: Choose Your Trustee**

Of all the decisions in estate planning, the selection of a successor trustee carries the most immediate and lasting practical consequence. It is also the decision most commonly deferred because it requires thinking carefully about real people in your life in ways that can feel uncomfortable—assessing their strengths and limitations honestly, considering how they would function under stress, acknowledging that the person you love most and the person best suited to this role may not be the same individual.

Within the next seven days, make this decision. Not a tentative mental note about who you're probably leaning toward, but an actual decision, written down, that you are prepared to name in a legal document. The person you choose as your successor trustee should be someone whose organizational reliability you trust completely, whose financial judgment you respect, who has enough time and proximity to do this work, and who you believe will honor your intentions even when that requires navigating family dynamics that may not be simple.

Once you've made the decision, have the conversation with the person you've chosen. This doesn't need to be a formal occasion. It is a direct, honest conversation in which you explain what the role involves, confirm their willingness to serve, and tell them where the documents will be located. Do the same with your chosen alternate. These conversations take thirty minutes each and provide something no document can substitute for: a person who steps into responsibility knowing they were chosen deliberately and understanding what that choice means.

If this decision surfaces genuine uncertainty—if you find yourself unable to identify anyone in your life who fits the profile, or if your family dynamics make any appointment feel like a minefield—write that uncertainty down and bring it to your attorney consultation. A professional trustee, a trust company, or a creative structural solution may be exactly what your situation requires, and knowing that a solution exists is more useful than remaining paralyzed by a problem you haven't yet explored.

While you're making the trustee decision, extend the same thinking to your healthcare agent and your financial power of attorney agent. These can be the same person as your successor trustee or different people, depending on who in your life is best suited to each role. By the end of the seven-day window, you should have names in mind for all three positions, even if those names remain subject to revision after your attorney consultation.

**Task Three: Schedule the Consultation**

The third task is the one that converts intention into a legal reality: schedule a consultation with an estate planning attorney. Not research an attorney. Not think about scheduling one. Schedule the appointment, with a specific date and time, before the seven days are up.

If you already have an estate planning attorney from a previous engagement, call or email their office and request a review consultation. Explain that you've been reassessing your plan and want to ensure your documents are current and complete. Most estate planning attorneys welcome these calls and can typically schedule an initial review within a few weeks.

If you don't have an existing relationship with an estate planning attorney, the most reliable path to finding a qualified one is through your state's bar association referral service, which maintains directories of attorneys by practice area and can connect you with someone licensed in your state. Personal referrals from a financial advisor, a CPA, or a trusted friend who has recently completed their own estate plan are equally reliable and have the advantage of coming with a firsthand account of the attorney's communication style and client experience.

When you contact the attorney's office, mention specifically that you are looking for help with a revocable living trust, a pour-over will, durable powers of attorney, and healthcare directives—the core document set this book has described. This specificity signals that you've done preliminary thinking and allows the office to estimate the scope of work accurately, which leads to a clearer fee discussion at the outset. Bring your document inventory and your trustee decisions to the consultation. You will cover more ground, receive more specific advice, and leave with a clearer action plan than the client who arrives without preparation.

The consultation itself is not the moment at which everything must be finalized. It is the moment at which a professional who knows the law in your state assesses your specific situation and tells you what your plan needs. That assessment is worth more than any amount of reading, because it is specific to you rather than general to a population, and because it translates understanding into a defined set of next steps that belong to your life rather than to an illustrative scenario in a book.

Momentum matters more than perfection. An imperfect plan, in place, serving your family is worth more than a comprehensive plan that exists only in intention. The three tasks above don't produce a perfect plan. They produce a beginning—one that an attorney can build from, that you can refine over time, and that provides more protection than anything you had before you started.

## 9.3 An Act of Love — What You're Really Leaving Behind

There is a reframing available to anyone who has read this far and still experiences estate planning as a morbid exercise—a necessary encounter with uncomfortable subjects best completed quickly and then set aside. It is a reframing that changes not just how estate planning feels but what it means to do it well.

Estate planning, at its most fundamental level, is not about death. It is about love expressed in a particular and irreplaceable form: the form of preparation.

Think about what the absence of a plan actually costs the people who survive you. It costs them time—months or years of probate administration during which they are managing paperwork and court appearances while simultaneously managing grief. It costs them money—the legal and administrative fees that consume a percentage of everything you worked to accumulate before a dollar reaches the people you intended to receive it. It costs them privacy—the public exposure of your financial life in court records that anyone can access. It costs them clarity—the absence of knowing what you actually wanted, which forces them to guess, or to fight, or to accept whatever the default rules of a legal system produce without reference to your specific intentions or your specific family.

And it costs them something harder to quantify but no less real: the experience of navigating the hardest season of their lives without the guidance you could have provided. Without the trust document that tells the successor trustee exactly what to do. Without the healthcare directive that tells the physicians exactly what you wanted. Without the legacy letter that tells your children exactly why you made the choices you made and what you hoped for them when you were gone. Without the critical contacts summary that tells whoever steps into your affairs exactly where to start.

The presence of a complete, current, well-communicated estate plan gives your family something that cannot be purchased after the fact and cannot be improvised in the middle of a crisis: it gives them clarity. And clarity, during the hardest season of a family's life, is one of the most generous gifts one person can give to another.

Consider what your family's experience looks like when the plan is in place. Your successor trustee knows they were chosen, knows where the documents are, and steps into a defined role with legal authority already established rather than scrambling for court authorization while a mortgage goes unpaid. Your healthcare agent knows your wishes in detail and can make decisions with confidence rather than guilt, knowing they are honoring what you wanted rather than guessing at it under the worst possible conditions. Your children know the shape of the plan, have heard your reasoning in your own words, and encounter no surprises that feel like betrayals—only the confirmation of what you told them, administered with the efficiency and privacy that a well-funded trust provides. Your grandchildren's inheritances are protected by the trust terms you specified, arriving at the ages and under the conditions you determined were right for them. Your spouse is financially secure. Your charitable intentions are honored. The assets you built are distributed to the people and causes that mattered to you, not to the administrative costs of a process you never intended.

This is not a fantasy outcome reserved for large estates managed by expensive attorneys. It is the ordinary result of ordinary planning done with ordinary care by people who decided that the people they love are worth the effort of preparation.

Estate planning carries the cultural weight of an uncomfortable subject because it requires looking directly at mortality—yours and others'—and making decisions in the presence of that acknowledgment. That discomfort is real, and it doesn't entirely disappear with reframing. But it sits alongside something equally real: the satisfaction of knowing that when the people you love most face the hardest moments of their lives, they will not face them alone in a probate court, fighting over an ambiguous document, uncertain about what you wanted, depleting the assets you worked decades to build on administrative processes you never intended to fund.

They will face those moments with clarity. With order. With the knowledge that you thought about them carefully enough, and loved them specifically enough, to prepare. That preparation is not a legal transaction. It is the final, most lasting expression of everything you built and everyone you loved throughout your life—translated into documents, yes, but rooted in something that no document created and no document can contain.

Margaret didn't get that chance. You do.

The work is not complicated. The tools are available. The people who can help you use them are a phone call away. What remains, as it has always remained, is simply the decision to begin—today, not eventually, not when things slow down, but now, while the full range of options is open and the people you love still have everything to gain from the choice you're about to make.

Begin today. Your family's future starts now.

www.ingramcontent.com/pod-product-compliance
Lightning Source LLC
LaVergne TN
LVHW022057200926
848481LV00003B/957
* 9 7 9 8 9 0 3 2 9 9 3 2 4 *